Chomsky for Activists

Those who regard him as a "doom and gloom" critic will find an unexpected Chomsky in these pages. Here the world-renowned author speaks in depth for the first time about his career in activism and his views on strategy and tactics. Chomsky offers new and intimate details about his life-long experience as an activist, revealing him as a critic with deep convictions and many surprising insights about movement strategies. The book points to new directions for activists today, including how the crises of the Coronavirus and the economic meltdown shaped the critical presidential election year and the organizing to come. Readers will find hope and new pathways toward a sustainable, democratic world.

Noam Chomsky is one of the most cited scholars in history and among the best known public intellectuals in the world today. He is the author of more than 100 books; the most recent include *Requiem for the American Dream: The 10 Principles of Concentration of Wealth and Power*. Before coming to the University of Arizona as Laureate Professor of Linguistics in 2017, Chomsky taught linguistics and philosophy at the Massachusetts Institute of Technology for 50 years.

Charles Derber, Professor of Sociology at Boston College is a noted public intellectual and author of 25 books, including several best-sellers reviewed in *The New York Times*, *The Washington Post*, *The Boston Globe*, and other prominent media. His recent books include *Welcome to the Revolution*, *Moving Beyond Fear*, and *Glorious Causes*. Co-editor of the Routledge book series *Universalizing Resistance*, Derber is a life-long activist for peace and justice.

Suren Moodliar is editor of the journal *Socialism and Democracy* and coordinator of encuentro5, a movement-building space in Downtown Boston. He is a co-author of *A People's Guide to Greater Boston*.

Paul Shannon worked for the American Friends Service Committee (AFSC) for 40 years where he ran the national film library and was active in various peace, union, prison reform, economic justice, and international solidarity movements. Now retired, he serves as a volunteer with the AFSC, teaches courses on the Vietnam war, writes, and continues his intersectional organizing around the Yemen war, the military industrial complex, climate change, criminal justice issues, and regime-change wars. He is a board member of Massachusetts Peace Action and the Campaign for Peace, Disarmament and Common Security.

"It is heartening to hear Chomsky's steady voice come through these interviews and writings — radical, analytic, and prophetic. *Chomsky for Activists* is the tonic we need in troubled times to peel away the illusions and fuel our fight for democracy, justice and economic equality."
Chuck Collins, Institute for Policy Studies, author,
The Wealth Hoarders and *Born on Third Base*

"Some people get to know the thinking of Noam Chomsky by listening to his presentations. But in this book you, the reader, have the opportunity to get to know the thinking of Chomsky in a different way. Through interviews as well as his commentaries, the reader gets a sense of the 'comprehensive' Chomsky. It is not just what he thinks but how he approaches the challenges facing the contemporary Left and progressive movements in the USA that makes this a compelling volume. This book is of additional value in identifying where the reader may agree and disagree with Chomsky, but nevertheless appreciate his invaluable insight. It was both a great honor and opportunity to have been asked to preview this volume in order to suggest to you, the potential reader, my encouragement that you embrace this work. You will not regret it!"
Bill Fletcher, Jr., executive editor,
globalafricanworker.com, former president
of TransAfrica Forum

"Could you benefit from a wise elder putting this present moment in historical perspective, explaining the gravity of today's existential crises but show-ing how activism has—and can—change the course of history for the better? Then curl up with Uncle Noam to read *Chomsky for Activists*. Chomsky gives simplistically brilliant answers to such questions as 'Is Trump a fascist?' (his response might surprise you) and 'Should we change the Democratic Party from within or create an independent party?'. *Chomsky for Activists* is an uplifting gift for all of us who feel de-pressed or confused about the state of our nation and world. Read it and act."

Medea Benjamin, Author and
Cofounder of CODEPINK

UNIVERSALIZING RESISTANCE SERIES
Edited by Charles Derber and Suren Moodliar

The series is publishing works by leading thinkers and activists developing the theory and practice of universalizing resistance. The books are written to engage professors, students, activists and organizers, and citizens who recognize the desperate urgency of a universalizing resistance that can mobilize the general population to build a new global society preserving life with justice.

International or Extinction (2020)
Noam Chomsky

Chomsky for Activists (2020)
Noam Chomsky

Forthcoming:

Revolution Has an Address! The Transformative Power of Movement Building Spaces
Suren Moodliar

For more information about this series, please visit: https://www.routledge.com/Universalizing-Resistance/book-series/RESIST

Chomsky for Activists

**Noam Chomsky,
Charles Derber,
Suren Moodliar,
Paul Shannon**

 Routledge
Taylor & Francis Group

NEW YORK AND LONDON

First published 2021
by Routledge
52 Vanderbilt Avenue, New York, NY 10017

and by Routledge
2 Park Square, Milton Park, Abingdon, Oxon, OX14 4RN

Routledge is an imprint of the Taylor & Francis Group, an informa business

© 2021 Taylor & Francis

The right of Noam Chomsky, Charles Derber, Suren Moodliar, Paul
Shannon to be identified as the authors of the editorial material, and of
the authors for their individual chapters, has been asserted in accordance
with sections 77 and 78 of the Copyright, Designs and Patents Act 1988.

Library of Congress Cataloging-in-Publication Data
Names: Chomsky, Noam, author. | Derber, Charles, author.
Title: Chomsky for activists / Noam Chomsky, Charles Derber, Suren
Moodliar, Paul Shannon.
Description: New York, NY: Routledge, 2021. |
Series: Universalizing resistance
Identifiers: LCCN 2020039030 | ISBN 9780367615864 (hardback) |
ISBN 9780367543396 (paperback) |
ISBN 9781003105619 (ebook)
Subjects: LCSH: Chomsky, Noam. | Social action—
United States. | Political participation—United States. | Political
activists—United States. |
United States—Politics and government.
Classification: LCC HN65 .C48 2021 | DDC 306.0973—dc23
LC record available at https://lccn.loc.gov/2020039030

ISBN: 978-0-367-61586-4 (hbk)
ISBN: 978-0-367-54339-6 (pbk)
ISBN: 978-1-003-10561-9 (ebk)

Typeset in Bembo
by codeMantra

Contents

Introduction

The political journalist, Alexander Cockburn, observed that the two greatest disasters to befall the American state in the 20th century both occurred on December 7th. One was Pearl Harbor in 1941; the other was the birth of Noam Chomsky in Philadelphia.[1] The events surrounding the former are the subject of continuing debate. The import of the latter, however, is beyond dispute for most of the left.

Rarely has a living intellectual commanded such widespread recognition both as an intellectual and as a citizen. Indeed, George Scialabba has described Chomsky as "America's most useful citizen."[2] Placing Cockburn and Scialabba in dialogue, one arrives at Chomsky's own formulation regarding the duty, not only of citizens but specifically of intellectuals and

1 Chomsky, Noam, and David Barsamian. *Global Discontents: Conversations on the Rising Threats to Democracy*. New York: Metropolitan Books, Henry Holt and Company, 2017.
2 Scialabba, George. "American Empire and Its Grim Wages." *Boston Globe*, April 25, 2004. http://archive. boston.com/ae/books/articles/2004/04/25/american_ empire_and_its_grim_wages/.

their "ownership" of the state that acts in their name and enables their work. As Chomsky concludes a recent edition of his classic, *The Responsibility of Intellectuals*, "Privilege yields opportunity; and opportunity confers responsibilities. An individual then has choices."[3] In the exercise of those choices, the intellectual is implored to challenge the prerogatives of the state and the party line, but they must also march alongside other concerned individuals in creating new, more emancipatory realities.

It is perhaps this *activist* function that has separated Chomsky from other intellectuals. That he is a public intellectual speaking to thousands is readily observed. But with the return of intellectuals as celebrities—think of Niall Ferguson, Yuval Noah-Harari, or Camille Paglia—what makes Chomsky different, apart from his political orientation, is that he has been largely excommunicated from the mainstream media. Among similarly afflicted left-wing intellectuals, Chomsky nevertheless stands out for his distinctive relationship to activism. He is at once viewed as doing the work that activists do, but never treated as such.

With this book, we hope to bring the activist Noam Chomsky, the one hiding in plain sight, to the fore. In doing so, we build on a companion volume, *Internationalism or Extinction*, which evoked the mood and *texture*

---

3 Chomsky, Noam. *The Responsibility of Intellectuals*. New York and London: The New Press, 2017.

of Chomsky's public lectures to convey the seriousness of the existential threats confronting humanity and set out the activist tasks that must be accomplished. In this sense, we want to go beyond the incomplete image of Chomsky as a relentless critic of US power to uncover the Chomsky who also offers a positive vision for social change and who is an exemplar of activism on many simultaneous planes.

Many years ago, the activist intellectual Cynthia Peters added to the conversation about Chomsky's relevance to activism with a comradely critique pithily formulated in an essay, "Talking Back to Chomsky."[4] Taking as a given that "our social-change movements have benefited enormously from the work of Noam Chomsky," she argues that there are three problems with Chomsky's advice to would-be activists given that they have an almost limitless choice of issues and organizations to join: (1) Chomsky's lack of attention to the problem of *proportionality*—the organizations that we can join are small and weak compared to the scale of the problems to be addressed; (2) *strategy*—we don't get a sense of where to invest our energies, i.e. Chomsky's talks don't identify the Empire's weaknesses; (3) *vision*—what should we demand?

Regarding proportionality, in this book and in many other conversations, Chomsky finds value in

---

4 Peters, Cynthia. "Talking Back to Chomsky." *Z Communications*, April 27, 2004. https://zcomm.org/zcommentary/talking-back-to-chomsky-by-cynthia-peters/.

the small groups addressing challenges in ways that correspond to their circumstances. He often draws on the experience of the revolutionary peasant-based Zapatistas in Mexico and their ability to network on a world scale to hold the Mexican state at bay. Another oft-cited example comes from social movements in Cochabamba, Bolivia, networking globally to defeat the Bechtel Corporation. Interestingly, Arundhati Roy adopted a similar posture standing alongside Chomsky at the World Social Forum in 2003 by declaring that "each in our own way," we have "laid siege to empire."[5] The claim here seems to be that modest organizations can achieve scale via networking.

A parallel claim can be made for strategy. Throughout this book one finds Noam allying with activist groups and refraining from a critique of their strategies. Instead, he is the faithful comrade, adding his voice to theirs—whether as a 10-year old writing about the fall of Barcelona, or a 40-year old blockading the Pentagon, or a 90-year old calling attention to (former Brazilian President) Lula's imprisonment. However, this does not mean that he is silent about strategy. One may discern his approach to strategy by examining his own practices. For example, Chomsky spends four to five hours a day answering e-mails. In generously sharing his leads and insights, as this

5 Roy, Arundhati. "Confronting Empire." *Ratical.org*, January 27, 2003. https://ratical.org/ratville/CAH/AR012703.html.

book's many personal reflections demonstrate, Noam is quite ecumenical in working with activists. Strategic breakthroughs—discovering where the Empire is weak or what issue or frame has traction—could emerge unpredictably from any one of the innumerable struggles he supports. What is critical then is that the successful examples be elevated and made available to the rest of humanity. And that is where Noam as a diligent communicator serves the movements strategically. For activists in his Boston-area hometown of many decades, Noam has provided a valuable repository of information on, and leads to, activists elsewhere on the planet.

As a critical node in the formal and informal global networks of activists, Noam is afforded a panoramic view of the world enabling him to identify strategically valuable and successful frames and repertoires of resistance. Of course, this is not an immediately helpful response to Peters' concern for strategy. It does not readily translate a view from 20,000 feet into a ground-level plan of action. But this is not reflective of Chomsky's limits, it is more an existential reality. Chomsky cannot be expected to know better than individuals and communities themselves what course of action best suits their needs. Deliberations within their communities and networks are likely the best places for authentic strategies to emerge.

To the degree that communication is important for communities and activists to make sense of their realities, Chomsky's work in challenging media monopolies as corporate entities provides another strategic insight for activists. He treats these behemoths as institutions with material practices and interests and as such they are knowable from a strategic point of view.[6] Armed with this framework, only the individual activist and her organization can determine the best entry point for agitation relative to their resources and capacities.

The "vision problem" may also find similar solution. For example, in the years after Evo Morales presidential victory in Bolivia, Chomsky would laud the former's reform agenda. Similarly, Chomsky sometimes embraces aspects of the secular nationalism that the United States represses in the Global South. He often chronicles and retells stories of the experiments in resistance and change that resonate with people in those countries. These are visions that Chomsky may not embrace for the United States but that have an authenticity for the partisans of those struggles. Vision is deeply historical and contextual and not readily portable from experience to experience. Indeed, similar laments are made about Karl Marx who offered socialism as a solution but with few exceptions refused to speculate about its content. This is the inherent paradox of "vision" in social change: it is supposed to be transcendental of a particular situation but is

6 Herman, Edward S., and Noam Chomsky. *Manufacturing Consent: The Political Economy of the Mass Media.* New York: Pantheon Books, 2002.

intimately tied to the peculiarities of that situation. No one-size-fits-all vision is available.

If the foregoing dialogue with the agenda set by Peters encourages the idea that Chomsky is a valuable resource for activists, it is our hope that this modest compendium corroborates that idea. In Part 1, by discussing his childhood with Paul Shannon, Chomsky reveals the personal circumstances of his North Philadelphia childhood that surely influenced his commitment to cause of the downtrodden. A Jewish boy in a predominantly German and Irish neighborhood found his ears attuned to global struggles, hearing echoes of the falls of Barcelona and Paris in the bullying and celebrations on his streets.

We also journey with him, literally following his footsteps across the historic Boston Common where tens of thousands would gather to hear his critique of US power in Vietnam. But we also take a walk with him, via Shannon's interview, back to those days, well before popular consciousness of US war crimes emerged. Those were lonely moments in which Chomsky spoke with everyone who would listen, be it in neighbor's living rooms or cold church basements. The speaker who today commands huge crowds not only began as a solitary agitator but he fortified his arguments and augmented their power in dialogue with activists. He started out as an *activist before* he became a leading interpreter of movements. What is all the more remarkable is that decades of acclaim for this activism has left his commitment to working horizontally with fellow activists undiminished as this book series testifies—a point made explicit in the concluding reflections from activists that constitutes Part 4.

After exploring episodes of Chomsky's activism, in Part 2 the book turns to broader reflections on many of the issues affecting our movements. These include some of the more divisive ones such as how to engage the electoral system. Recently, for example, Chomsky has called on third parties to stand down in the US presidential election lest Trump be re-elected.[7] This is consistent with his position on earlier elections in which Chomsky advocated a "safe-state" strategy wherein people voted for third parties in states where such votes would not determine the allocation of that state's electoral votes. The rationale for this position is explored in Part 2—not only relative to the electoral framework but also in terms of a vision for the left as a whole. Its base is *not* in the electoral sphere, instead it is rooted in social movements. Here too Chomsky as a visionary activist surfaces—this time as one who imagines a left that can engage with evangelicals, a hypothesis firmly rooted in history. Similarly, Chomsky refuses to prioritize among social movements and their diverse claims. Instead, facing the credible and imminent threats to human survival, he calls on social

---

7   TruthDig. "An Open Letter to the Green Party for 2020." January 24, 2020. https://www.truthdig.com/articles/an-open-letter-to-the-green-party-for-2020/.

movements to integrate activism on global concerns with their particular struggles rather than choosing between them. A sharp focus on working-class issues and labor organizing provides the universalizing "glue" that can help these movements cohere, especially in an era in which the US working class has been feminized and people of color are increasingly exercising leadership from within its ranks.

The prospects for these movements are explored in Part 3 in the context of 2020 as an election year in the "most powerful state in world history." Declaring that this may be "the most important election in human history," Chomsky provides analysis of the stakes in light of the conflation of Trump's fate with those of leading corporate interests, "the masters of the universe." Whether this holds or business interests decide to ditch the deadly Trump circus remains an open question. Necessarily, Chomsky investigates the origins and impact of the COVID-19 pandemic afflicting humanity as a whole while unmasking the "pathology of capitalist logic." Against the deadly virus, deep depression, growing authoritarianism, and existential threats, Chomsky nonetheless finds inspiration in youth movements and the global left—appealing to Gramsci's injunction for a "pessimism of intellect, optimism of will."

Humanity's volition, their capacity to understand and change the world, is explored by Chomsky through several avenues of inquiry. Indeed, one of the best places for readers to understand the philosophical underpinnings of Chomsky's linguistic, philosophical, and political investigations is an accessible, short book, *What Kinds of Creatures Are We?*[8] In Part 4, however, we learn *What Kind of Person Noam Chomsky Is.* The authors approached a dozen activist thinkers who have worked with Chomsky over the years to learn how he has impacted their activism. Some shared the brief anecdotes requested, others shared tributes. Underlying them all is common theme—*Noam* has made himself available to the movement with astonishing generosity. Although this is a Chomsky that is rarely highlighted in interviews, one that Noam seems to treat as a distraction from the matters of global concern, it is clearly one that emerges while working with others to change the world. In this individual and with these kinds of collaborations, we can understand why a disaster befell the American imperial state on December 7, 1928.

8   Chomsky, Noam. *What Kind of Creatures Are We?* Columbia Themes in Philosophy. New York: Columbia University Press, 2016.

Part 1

Reflections on a Life of Activism

I was a 10-year-old kid... There was real fear of the rise of fascism in Europe, which was personalized by the fact that in my own [Philadelphia] neighborhood... it was right around me. The Germans and the Irish Catholics were pro-Nazi. I remember beer parties when Paris fell. Just being a kid on the streets, interacting with other kids. I mean, it wasn't like now. You're not going to get murdered. No shootings, no knifings, but it was difficult and unpleasant.

It was also pretty tense because we were getting involved in really direct open resistance and expecting long jail sentences. But there was also a mass public opposition by 1968–1969 getting a million people demonstrating. For years, my recollection of Washington, my sense of Washington was tear gas and mace because that's what was going on.

I was there [in 1971] with a group of what were called older people. We were maybe [in our] '40s. Howard [Zinn], Marilyn Young, Dan Ellsberg. We were a small affinity group and we were trying to get arrested, and they wouldn't arrest us because they only wanted to arrest young people. So, you sit in the middle of the street and police cars are racing toward you, but they swerve right around you, and meanwhile some kid walking with jeans on the sidewalk, they'd pick him up.

1 How It All Got Started

Noam Chomsky, Charles Derber,
Suren Moodliar, and Paul Shannon

So, we figured we could have a march from Harvard to the Boston Common, the normal place for meetings, and have a demonstration at the Boston Common. The march went okay. There was a huge police presence, state police, in the Common. We got to the bandstand. A couple speakers got up. I was one of the speakers. You couldn't hear a word. We were drowned out by counter-demonstrators, many of them students marching in from the universities. The police protected people like us from being murdered.

PAUL: So Noam, you have spent most of the last 50 or 60 years in this area, in Greater Boston. And people—especially outside of this area—have an image of Boston as kind of a very liberal and pro-peace place to live. I wonder if you could talk about what it was like for you and for others back in the mid-'60s, trying to engage in actions in Boston related to the war or civil rights or other issues.

NOAM: Well, let's take civil rights. There was strong support for the Civil Rights Movement as long as it was focusing on racist sheriffs in Alabama. Then, a lot of outrage, anger, how could they do these terrible things, and so on. When you listen to the rhetoric on Martin Luther King's Day, it ends with "I have a dream." He didn't stop there. He went on to the North, to try to organize a Poor People's Movement that took pretty radical positions. He was assassinated, after all, when he was in Memphis to support a sanitation worker strike. He was on his way to Washington, he hoped, to organize a Resurrection City, a big demonstration, and lay the basis for a Poor People's Movement—black and white.

As soon as he started on that, his appeal to northern liberals sharply declined. He also came out strongly against the Vietnam War. Not early, incidentally, later on, but even that was held against him. That part of his career, which for him was the peak of his career, was not just about voting rights for blacks in the South. That's almost wiped out of the legacy. The reason is it just was not acceptable to northern liberals. We could go into how when school desegregation was implemented in Boston, notice how it was done by liberal leaders. It was done so as to exclude the affluent white suburbs and to integrate Irish and black areas. That's a recipe for race riots.

An Irish guy working for a telephone company gets a small house, lives in a community with his friends, and wants to send his kid to the local high school, cheer for the football team. This is taken away from him. Now his kid has to go to a black area, a black kid comes to his area. While in the affluent suburbs, you cluck your tongue about the racism of the Boston Irish. I mean, that's a model for the way it was done, in Boston and around the country. That's the Civil Rights Movement. In fact, well, we know the outcomes.

Let's go back to the anti-war movement. Boston is a liberal city. The war escalated. The war was going on in the 1950s. Maybe 60,000 or 70,000 people were killed in South Vietnam under the highly brutal, repressive government the United States was supporting. No protest. Nobody even noticed. In 1961 and 1962, Kennedy sharply escalated the war. He ordered US planes to start bombing South Vietnam. It was under South Vietnamese markings, but everybody knew they were US planes. He authorized napalm. He began programs of chemical warfare for crop destruction and livestock destruction, part of an effort to drive much of the population into what amounted to concentration camps or urban slums. This was a sharp escalation.

You couldn't talk about it. I mean, I was giving talks then where I'd ask somebody if they could invite a couple of people to their living room, and we could talk to maybe four or five people. That was a talk. Or maybe some church where they'd let three or four people in to have a meeting, basically nothing. There were a few meetings at the universities, if we tried. A couple of us were concerned. We wanted MIT or Harvard, in the early 1960s, to have a discussion that would bring in Vietnam. You had to bring in 10 other topics, one of them being Vietnam, and then maybe you could get a couple of people to listen to it.

It was beginning to change by the mid-1960s. In February 1965, the United States began bombing North Vietnam. That became an issue, the idea that you're bombing another country. South Vietnam was fair game. In fact, almost the entire world was against South Vietnam, but that's okay. We're allowed to do what we want in South Vietnam. The illusion is we're defending the people. We're actually attacking them, and the people who really knew about the war like Bernard Fall were very clear and frank about this. The bombing of North Vietnam did raise issues. For one thing, it might bring in the Russians, it might bring in the Chinese, dangerous and so on. It was beginning to become possible to talk about the bombing of North Vietnam.

Liberal intellectuals and scientists were advocating a barrier that would prevent North Vietnamese from coming to the south to support South Vietnamese guerrillas the United States was attacking. That was considered a super liberal idea, because it would then allow us to attack South Vietnam without any interference. That was the mentality, kind of, on the left. I remember these proposals being made to me, saying,

"Look, you shouldn't oppose what our government's doing, because look how progressive it is."

Now, internationally there was a protest movement. And on October 15, 1965 there was an international day of protest. By that time, South Vietnam had been half destroyed. Hundreds of thousands of American troops were pouring into the country. The bombing of North Vietnam had gone on for months. It was a pretty big issue by then.

So, we figured we could have a march from Harvard to the Boston Common, the normal place for meetings, and have kind of a demonstration at the Boston Common. The march went okay. There was a huge police presence, state police, in the Common. We got to the bandstand. A couple speakers got up. I was one of the speakers. You couldn't hear a word. We were drowned out by counter-demonstrators, many of them students marching in from the universities. The police protected people like us from being murdered. Not because they liked us, but they just didn't want bloodshed in the Boston Common. Take a look at the Boston Globe the next day, probably most of the liberal papers in the country: bitter denunciations of what happened—denunciations namely of the demonstrators! How could they dare to say we shouldn't bomb North Vietnam, and shouldn't support our glorious country, and so on. That was 1965.

The second international day of protest was March 1966. We figured we can't have something on the

Common. We'll have it in church. We had a meeting in the Arlington Street Church, right near the
Common. The church was attacked by demonstrators
throwing cans and tomatoes and defacing the church.
That was March 1966. That's Boston.

Take a look at Congress. The liberal Congress-
men who later presented themselves as anti-war—
figures like Mike Mansfield and others—were
bitterly condemning the demonstrators in April of
1966. Now back in 1965, April of 1965, Howard
Zinn and two or three other people decided to call
ourselves the Delegation of New England Professors
and go down to Washington to lobby our representatives. It was pretty interesting. The senior senator,
Saltonstall, invited us into his office. We had a po-
lite conversation. At the end, he looked at us, and
he said, "I really don't understand what you're doing here. The president has spoken." In fact, he had
given a speech saying we're sending a couple hundred thousand more troops, so what more is there to
talk about?

We went to see Tip O'Neill, later considered a
great anti-war activist. He literally wouldn't let us
into his office. He didn't want to have these Com-
mie rats spoiling his office. We actually talked to
Ted Kennedy, the junior senator. He was very ac-
commodating, even invited us to lunch in the Sen-
ate dining room, but said, "I really don't know
much about this kind of business. Foreign affairs is
my brother's concern. It may be interesting, but not

interesting to me." That's what it was like in the mid–1960s.

PAUL: People don't know that.

NOAM: A year or two later, it changed, but it was a struggle.

PAUL: Now, you're talking about getting involved in these demonstrations in the mid-60s. When was the first demonstration or protest event that you went to in your life?

NOAM: In my life?

PAUL: Yes.

NOAM: Well, I mean, I wasn't actively involved in the Civil Rights Movement, but I did go down there. They had a big demonstration in Jackson, Mississippi, which was pretty brutal and bloody.

PAUL: Where did you grow up?

NOAM: Philadelphia, in a place where I was scared to death of people like you, literally. It was the Irish kids down the block who were really frightening.

PAUL: Yeah, you were afraid for a good reason.

NOAM: They went to the local Catholic school. They were violently anti-Semitic. We were the only Jewish family in the area, so I carefully avoided the Irish kids. It took me a long time to get over it.

PAUL: Your parents were very smart in giving you that advice. When did you start thinking in terms of the direction the country was going?

NOAM: It was very early. In fact, my wife, Valeria, and I were in Barcelona watching television on November 8th when the news was coming in about the (2016) election. Which, for me, had a significant personal element to it. The first article I remember writing was in February 1939, right after the fall of Barcelona to Franco. The article, I'm sure, was not very memorable. I was a 10-year-old kid.

PAUL: You were 10 years old?

NOAM: It was about the rise of fascism in Europe: Austria, Germany, Toledo in Spain, and Barcelona. It looked as if its spread is inexorable, like it's going to go all over everywhere. That was the '30s. There was real fear of the rise of fascism in Europe, which was personalized by the fact that in my own neighborhood where I lived...

PAUL: In Philadelphia...

NOAM:... it was right around me. The German and the Irish Catholics were pro-Nazi. I remember beer parties when Paris fell. Just being a kid on the streets, interacting with other kids. I mean, it wasn't like now. You're not going to get murdered. No shootings, no knifings, but it was difficult and unpleasant to be with kids like you. Scary kids.

SUREN MOODLIAR: Noam, how, at 10 years old, did you find out about what was happening in Spain?

NOAM: I could read the newspapers. Actually, I was spending time going to the Philadelphia Public Library, big public library, where they happened to have a tremendous collection of radical publications. I was reading things, you know, by the time I was 11 or 12 and picked things up a little bit myself. Also I had family in New York, mostly Jewish unemployed, pretty radical, very activist. My aunts, who would come visit, were members of the International Ladies' Garment Workers Union and kind of left activists. So it was kind of all around.

PAUL: So your family came out of...

NOAM: Not my immediate family.

SUREN MOODLIAR: So you had extended family in New York.

NOAM: I had uncles and aunts and cousins in New York, where I would go as soon as I got old enough to take the train by myself—around 12 years old. I'd go there any time I had a chance. I used to hang around—it's not there anymore—but Union Square used to be a center for radical offices. The '30s were a pretty lively period. Down

Fourth Avenue, there were small bookstores. A lot of them were run by emigres, and some of them by emigres from Spain, Spanish anarchists who'd fled. They were interested there in the Yiddish anarchists office of the *Freie Arbeiter Stimme*. It was in Union Square. It wasn't ordinary for a kid to come in and want to talk to people and pick up pamphlets. So a lot of people were willing to talk and give me materials. In fact, I still have a lot of the stuff I picked up from them.

PAUL: When did your critique of US foreign policy begin?

NOAM: Right away. It was clear—I didn't actually know it until about 1940 or '41—but information from the late '30s made it quite clear that the United States was tacitly supporting Franco. It was denied by the State Department at the time and never made it to the press. Later, it was conceded. It was reported in the Left press. What happened was that Franco was being supported openly by the Nazis and the Fascists, the Germans and the Italians. The West had an embargo against Spain. The one commodity that the Fascists couldn't get from Germany and Italy was oil. The Texaco oil company, which at the time was run by an open Nazi, diverted its tankers from the Republic to the Fascists. The Left press reported it. The US government claimed it wasn't happening. Yes, it was happening. If you read the Left press, you knew about it.

Children from Republican families preparing for evacuation from Spain during the Spanish Civil War (1936-39).
Photo from Wikipedia Commons, photographer unknown.

Meanwhile, Roosevelt was bitterly condemning some businessmen who had sold a couple of pistols to the Republic for violating the embargo. Meanwhile, the Texaco oil company was radically violating the embargo by providing the Fascist armies with the one thing they needed and couldn't get. Things like that were happening. If you looked hard, you could find them. If you hung around the right circles, you could get the pamphlets and newspapers and even people who knew of them.

PAUL: Did you and those in your circle....

NOAM: There was no circle.

PAUL:... support World War II? What was the attitude at that point?

NOAM: I mean, my own feeling was that the war could have been prevented. Once it took place, okay, it's a war that I thought had to be fought once it took place. There was no circle, incidentally, maybe two or three people you could talk to. I was pretty critical of a lot of things that were going on. For example, my high school, this is the early '40s now, happened to be right next to a prisoner of war camp where they had German prisoners of war. There was just kind of barbed wire in-between. The kids would go out there during recess and scream at the Germans. You know, curses. A couple of us tried to say, "Look, they're just people like us who were caught up in the war. They don't deserve any of this behavior." It was only two or three of us.

When the British conquered Greece in 1944, it was pretty brutal. In fact, Churchill's orders were to treat Athens as a conquered city. One of the things that the Americans and British were doing as they entered southern Europe was destroying the resistance. Their main enemy was the anti-Fascist resistance. They tried to restore the traditional order. You didn't know a lot of it then. You could see some of it at the time. A lot came out later. In Greece, it was very striking. I was very critical of that.

I couldn't stand the anti-Japanese propaganda. If you go back and look at it—John Dower has an interesting book where he collects a lot of it—the Germans were treated with a certain respect. They're, after all, blond, Aryan, good people, but the Japanese were treated just like vermin. "They're not even human. Just crush them. Destroy them." It was pretty open. Even before Pearl Harbor, it was open. Before Pearl Harbor, the Japanese could read in American newspapers comments and discussions by leading figures about how we have to build up a big air force to attack Japan so we can burn down the ant heaps where these vermin live, and so on and so forth. By our standards, the Japanese attack on Pearl Harbor was justified. By OUR standards.

Then in the early post-war period, the anti-Communism developed very quickly and became total hysteria long before McCarthy. It was really hard to combat it.

PAUL: I've often wondered to myself, do you have any idea how many talks you've given?

NOAM: I know during the late '60s, it was sometimes half a dozen a day. Just constant. It's tailed off....

PAUL: It's tailed off?

NOAM: ...a lot. My wife doesn't agree.

PAUL: Well, I just remember in the '70s, certainly, you and Howard Zinn spoke an awful lot together.

NOAM: We had one very memorable talk together. It was in April 1975. We were on panels together many times, but we happened to be on a panel at Brandeis University. Right in the middle of I think Howard was talking, a kid ran down the aisle yelling, "The war's over!"

PAUL: April 30th, yes.

NOAM: He and I were a good pair, because we had very different styles and very different manner. It worked very well.

PAUL: What was it like for you when Howard died?

NOAM: He was a good friend. Almost as soon as he came to Boston, we became friends. That Jackson, Mississippi thing, we went down together.

Bunker Hill Community College, Boston, September 27, 2004. Howard Zinn and Noam Chomsky.
Photo by Roger Leisner.

PAUL: I only found out after he died that Howard was a big baseball fan. Did you and he ever go to a game together or do that type of thing?

NOAM: No.

PAUL: No? Not your thing?

NOAM: I was a baseball fan, too, but in the '30s.

PAUL: What about that?

NOAM: What about that?

PAUL: Yeah. It was important to you?

NOAM: You really want to be bored? I can take you inning after inning through the first baseball game I saw in 1937, the A's and the Yankees.

PAUL: At Yankee Stadium?

NOAM: No, no, I was in Philadelphia.

PAUL: Oh yes, the Philadelphia A's.

NOAM: Philadelphia, sorry.

PAUL: Not the Oakland or Kansas City A's.

NOAM: Right, Philadelphia A's. It was very tough for kids in Philadelphia, Jewish kids, because our cousins were all in New York, and New York won the championship in everything and Philadelphia was last in everything. But I did manage to sit right behind Joe DiMaggio in the cheap seats in the center field bleachers during the... I won't bore you with the details of the game. The As were actually winning until the seventh inning when the Yankees got seven runs and won 10 to seven.

SUREN MOODLIAR: Did you go to other games, too?

NOAM: No, it was too expensive. It cost a quarter. Couldn't do that.

PAUL: Could you follow on the radio?

NOAM: To this game I went to only because my fourth grade teacher took me and my best friend as kind of a present.

PAUL: Your interest in sports kind of diminished as time went on?

NOAM: Well, professional sports. It's kind of fun. One of my grandsons was a jock for a year or two, and I'd take him to professional games. It was fun.

PAUL: I do want to just ask one last question. Noam, you're not as young as you used to be.

NOAM: Really?

PAUL: When events take place, at least in this area, and I assume in other areas too, it's amazing how many of the audience are young people. I mean, it's over-whelmingly. What do you attribute that to?

NOAM: I think it's a very good sign. You could even see it in the voting. Among voters under 25, this pro-Sanders vote was overwhelming across the spectrum. I think like 75% or something. There's a lot of young people who are active. I think activism today is higher than it was in the peak of the '60s. You know, it's not as focused and dramatic, but it's all over the place. A lot of people are really concerned with deeply important issues. That's a big change from the '50s and '60s.

PAUL: Especially from 1965.

NOAM: I'm not afraid of the Irish kids anymore.

Closing: The last visit to Boston Common

It was also pretty tense because we were getting involved in really direct open resistance and expecting long jail sentences. But there was also a mass public opposition by 1968–69 getting a million people demonstrating. For years, my recollection of Washington, my sense of Washington was tear gas and mace because that's what was going on.

PAUL: Noam, we're heading toward the famous bandstand here on Boston Common where you have spoken numerous times for so many important organizing efforts around peace and social justice. This will probably be your last visit to the bandstand since you'll be moving out of the area very shortly. Do you remember when the last time was that you spoke here?

NOAM: The last time?

PAUL: Yeah.

NOAM: All through the '80s. It was very different then from in the mid-60's

PAUL: Yes?

NOAM: It's interesting, there was a tremendous switch from '66 to '67. It was completely different.

PAUL: People started to… The combination of things going horribly in Vietnam and the fact that the word was out about what was going on in Vietnam.

NOAM: Somehow a fire. The kindling must have been ready, and something sparked it.

PAUL: Yeah. The same thing kind of happened in Iraq around 2005, 2006, though, remember?

NOAM: Yeah. But remember, in Iraq there was a huge demonstration right before, the day before the war.

PAUL: That's true.

NOAM: I remember I had two classes at MIT and students in both classes insisted on canceling the classes to come down for the demonstration, which we did of course.

PAUL: Then there was a lot of support for the war, once we actually went in for a few years. But then little things started to arouse opposition, like

Cindy Sheehan setting her little stand up outside of Bush's ranch.

NOAM: Abu Ghraib.

PAUL: The news on Abu Ghraib.

NOAM: Yeah.

PAUL: So this is the famous bandstand, soon to be called "The Noam Chomsky bandstand". No?

NOAM: "The Howard Zinn Bandstand".

PAUL: Yeah. Howard gave some great speeches here too.

NOAM: He was a great public speaker.

PAUL: Yeah. Well you both played off of each other so well though.

NOAM: Yeah we really did.

PAUL: Who were some of the people back then that come to mind that you worked with?

NOAM: Well, the first one here was Russ Johnson, did you know him?

PAUL: Of course. Yeah.

NOAM: He was great. Then when he left, Howard came along. Who else?

PAUL: You spoke a number of times with George Wald, I believe.

NOAM: George was in 1969 but I think it was at a university setting. He gave a very passionate speech on March 4th in MIT, which galvanized a lot of students.

PAUL: I remember that. Yes. What do you think were the key events during that period of time in the '60s and '70s?

NOAM: By late 1966 early '67 the resistance movement was just beginning—draft resistance. October 1967 was the draft card turn-in at Arlington Street Church. Then we went down to the Pentagon: The big Pentagon demonstration, which got a lot of publicity, and the draft card turn-in at the Justice Department, which led to the Spock-Coffin trial—picking all the wrong people—for prosecution, which was kind of a farce.

So, for example, I was a co-conspirator in the trial and the reason I wasn't a conspirator was that the two events that they picked to make you a conspirator were being at a press conference, and physically turning in the draft cards. I was at the press conference, but I didn't physically turn in draft cards because I was giving a talk arranging the crowd outside.

PAUL: Purely coincidental.

NOAM: So I was only a co-conspirator.

Spock and Coffin had almost nothing to do with it. In fact, they could never get the Jewish names straight.

So they mixed up Mark Raskin and Art Roscoe who were both furious because Mark didn't want to be conspirator and Art did want to be one. It was something to see. The things that were going on then were wild.

PAUL: How did that feel when, all of the sudden, there was this upsurge in opposition almost out of nowhere?

NOAM: It was also pretty tense because we were getting involved in really direct open resistance and expecting long jail sentences. But there was also a mass public opposition by 1968–69 getting a million people demonstrating. For years, my recollection of Washington, my sense of Washington was tear gas and mace because that's what was going on.

PAUL: You were at that, what was it 1971, with the mass civil disobedience in Washington?

NOAM: I was there with a group of what were called older people. We were maybe in our '40s. Howard, Marilyn Young, Dan Ellsberg. We were a small affinity group and we were trying to get arrested, and they wouldn't arrest us because they only wanted to arrest young people. So you sit in the middle of the street and police cars are racing toward you, but they swerve right around you, and meanwhile some kid walking with jeans on the sidewalk, they'd pick him up.

Antiwar group in Washington, D.C., 1971. Marilyn B. Young is on the far left, Howard Zinn is in the middle, and Daniel Ellsberg and Noam Chomsky are seated to the right of Zinn.

PAUL: There were thousands of arrests.

NOAM: And most of them were people who had nothing to do with it. The ones who were trying to get arrested couldn't.

Howard finally got himself arrested and maced. I remember Dan treated our little group like his marine platoon, "let's go over here, it's more exciting." It was quite a scene.

What really changed things enormously was the Tet Offensive in January 1968. It just changed everything. It was an amazing uprising. If you take a look at the Pentagon papers, they end in mid-1968, and the last couple of pages discuss the government proposal, the Johnson proposal to send another couple hundred thousand troops to South Vietnam after the offensive. The Joint Chiefs were opposed because they said they would need them for civil disorder control in the United States. Because there would be such a blow out if they sent those new troops. That's what the state of the country was like.

Then in 1970 when Nixon invaded Cambodia, the place just totally exploded. Even liberal elites going crazy.

PAUL: Did you have, in that period of time, a network of people who would stay in touch with each other about what events to do or how to respond?

NOAM: I was mainly connected with the resistance. The organization, Resist, was formed then and a group of people, friends mostly, we worked together on a lot of things not just antiwar, but also support for the Panthers and other things. I remember January '69, I guess it was, I flew out to Chicago for the Fred Hampton funeral. Was probably the only white face in the audience, but we were working with Panthers and other groups and so it spread.

PAUL: Just constant activity

NOAM: It was very constant

Oh yeah, I remember days when I did seven or eight talks a day, race around. We're also facing probable jail sentence so people's plans changed.

My first wife Carol went back to school. She'd been away for 16 years because we figured...

{Suddenly lawn sprinklers near the bandstand go off, spraying Noam and Paul}—

NOAM: [laughing] Oh, wow, better get out of here. They have a new technique instead of tear gas or mace. Now they use hidden sprinklers.

PAUL: {back in a dry area} So Carol went back to teaching?

NOAM: Back to school to get her degree. She had been away for 16 years. We had a couple of kids.

Looked like I'd be in jail. So pretty tense period, but a very exciting. Lot of things going on.

PAUL: Was that period the high point of your work in Boston, or did that come later?

NOAM: Well, that was the highpoint of activism, but I never really liked it. I never liked to give public talks up here. Howard was very good at it, but I did it reluctantly. But it just had to be done.

PAUL: How many times do you think you spoke here?

NOAM: Probably four or five. And a number of times at one of the churches right over there...

PAUL: Yes, St. Paul's up the street there-

NOAM: St. Paul's, yeah. That's where we went after the Iraq demonstration. Instead of classes at MIT, we all went over there. One of the many times. Then the Arlington Street Church down that way.

PAUL: What do you think was the largest demonstration that you were at here at the Common?

NOAM: Must have been... it kind of all blends. I don't know... Must have been around '68, '69. Those are the big ones. Then again, during the Central American Wars there were demonstrations on Nicaragua and things like that. Arrests and so on. Sit ins. It was a long, long period.

PAUL: What mistakes do you think that whole movement made after '75 when the war ended?

NOAM: Well, by 1969, the student movement which was kind of the cutting edge, just fractured. One group went off to be Weatherman, which was suicidal and self-destructive. The other group became Maoist, which was also suicidal and self destructive. Things just fractured. Even May Day in 1971 was—I went because you sort of had to go—kind of crazy. They're not going to occupy Washington.

PAUL: Given all that happened and how different the situation is in some ways today, what lessons should we learn today from what happened after that huge movement fractured?

NOAM: Well, you should learn that the movements that were really successful were those that organized and educated and acted nonviolently on issues. As soon as they move to adventurist tactics like the Weathermen, it was just self destructive. In fact, I remember meetings with the Vietnamese where they were pleading with people here not to do those things because they didn't care about how people here felt about themselves. They wanted to survive, and it was obvious that those tactics were just breaking up the anti-war activity, which of course it did. I think that lesson still holds.

PAUL: Do you feel that what we're doing right now, with these large demonstrations that come out every now and then usually protesting the Alt-Right right—are what we're doing now accomplishing what has to be done to build an effective movement?

NOAM: It's a mixture. When it moves to what they call preemption, you know blocking talks, I think that's harmful. It's a gift to the right. When it moves to initiating violence, which is different from self-defense, it's a gift to the far-right, they love it. It's kind of like Weatherman's breaking windows on Main Street. It's great for the right-wing, Nixon loved it, and it's terrible for the victims. When you can really approach people saying, "Look, here. We understand your problems, they're real, and here's a solution to them. Let's work on that," that can be done.

Like what happened in Central America was amazing, the Central American Movement was something totally new in the history of Imperialism. Nothing like it. It was the first time ever—this never gets discussed—it was the first time ever in the history of Imperialism that people from the Imperial country not only protested the atrocities but went to live with the victims. Nobody ever dreamt of that in Vietnam. You didn't go to a Vietnamese village, and in the Algerian war nobody went and lived in an Algerian village.

Thousands of people went, and who were they? Evangelical Christians, rural churches, people in Kansas. Those are the people who were going down there and working with and protecting the victims. That hasn't disappeared.

PAUL: So it's pretty important that we connect up with folks like that?

NOAM: Definitely. I remember going to churches in rural Maryland and Kansas where people knew more about Central America than the activist movements because they'd been there.

PAUL: Yes, that was an amazing time.

Let me just ask one more thing.

Given that there's so much polarization out there, and given the need to hook-up with people and relate to people of different backgrounds, what are we doing now that really is helpful along those lines, and what are we doing that undermines that goal?

NOAM: Quite a lot. So for example, my wife and I were in Arizona last winter, and one of the things we did was go on a trip to the border with some of the No More Deaths groups, which set up camps in the desert to try to help the migrants who are dying in the deserts. Some groups are finding many dead bodies in the desert. They work with the medical bureau trying to link them up with relatives so at least people know what happened to their cousin and son and so on. These are activities that bring in a lot of people and a lot of support. People understand that. That's what you can do.

I remember meetings with the Vietnamese where they were pleading, as I said, not to carry out the violent attacks, and what they advised were things so mild that activists here laughed at it. They said what really impressed them was when a group of women went to a cemetery and prayed at the graves of American soldiers. That, they felt, was really great because that would reach people, get them to understand what's going on, and go beyond that and say, "It's not just American soldiers, it's also those Vietnamese are being murdered." That works.

2 Stories of Global Activism

Noam Chomsky, Charles Derber,
Suren Moodliar, and Paul Shannon

Well, the most hopeful experiences I've had are involvement with the really poor and deprived people who were struggling and achieving. I visited an extremely poor village in Southern Colombia that was miles from the nearest road—only could get to it through an almost impassable dirt road. On the way, there's a small graveyard with crosses where people were murdered by paramilitaries. In the village themselves, [people were] very friendly, warm, inviting you in. They were struggling against an effort by miners to destroy what would amount to their water supply. Watching people like that, they actually did something. The reason I went was because I had been in southern Colombia a number of times to the conflicted areas.

My late wife died 10 years ago. They were setting up a memorial for her on the top of the nearby mountain. We all climbed up the mountain. There were shamans, and they had a ceremony, and put up a plaque. It was part of their effort to protect the virgin forest and the mountain and the water supply from miners. The first time I was supposed to go, we couldn't go because there was too much violence in the area. Then, there happened to be a period of quiet. These people are really dedicated. The kind of human sympathy that you just don't see in many places. That's the kind of thing that's inspiring. I've seen that all over the world.

PAUL: …. Noam, when did you start actually giving talks, public talks like you give today?

NOAM: In the '40s.

PAUL: That early?

NOAM: Yeah, but it was on different issues. The issue I was really concerned with at the time was Palestine. I was involved with small but not totally insignificant groups that were what was called Zionist at the time, would be called anti-Zionist now, who were opposed to a Jewish state. They were supporting a Jewish-Arab working class co-operation to build a socialist Palestine, which was part of the Zionist movement, at the time, incidentally, believe it or not. Then, I was very active in that, organizing youth groups and talks, all sorts of things. Just for fun in 1948, I wrote an article supporting Henry Wallace's candidacy. But I wrote it in Arabic, because I was learning Arabic at the time. I wish I still had it.

PAUL: Not too many pieces like that around.

SUREN: I read an interview with you about left Zionism and the fact that it was only in, I think, 1942 when a call emerged for a state of Israel or a call for a state in the first place……

NOAM: First of all, it's true that the first official commitment of the Zionist movement to a Jewish state was in 1942, but it was latent before that. It was in the background of the minds of many people, and it was opposed by many Zionists.

But then you had other things happening. You had the war, you had the Holocaust. Huge blows were struck that changed the calculation completely. As late as 1946, I guess, the Anglo-American Commission, still about 25% of the Jews in Palestine were opposed to a Jewish state. So, it was not negligible. There were political movements like Hashomer Hatzair, which was officially committed to bi-nationalism.

There were other more activist groups which I was personally associated with which went much further, calling for socialist Palestine. But they were kind of wiped out by the juggernaut of political Zionism supported by major powers to try to create a state that... They didn't call it a Jewish state in those days, but a state which would be basically Jewish. Then, of course, came the war and expulsions. You just had a different situation.

SUREN: To step back a little in the timeline. Prior to 1942, then, the call for a state was somewhat latent, perhaps, and there were also those who rejected the call for a state?

NOAM: First of all, the Zionist movement, all together, was a tiny minority of Jews. Go back in time to the first World War, I think maybe something like 1% of the world Jewish population had a Zionist, what they called a Shekel, member. Remember that the bulk of the Jewish population was in Eastern Europe, and they were just exterminated. That made a huge difference. They were mainly anti-Zionists, labor-based, and so on. So, they just wiped out the population and, of course, that changed everything.

SUREN: Would you say that left Zionism, then, in that period before the Holocaust, that it was a form of nationalism without the goal of a state?

NOAM: Well, depends who you were asking. The leadership definitely had a state in mind. They didn't want to talk about it because that would have been... The lesson of Zionism, which, actually, the Palestinians should learn, is, "Don't say what you're doing. Just do it." Little bits and pieces. So, the slogan was Dunam, after the term, "dunam." A dunam's like a quarter of an acre or so. Just take a little piece here and there—but do it quietly. The actual terminology is so that the *Goyim* don't notice. So, you go to a hill, and you put up a little outpost, and then you put a house near it. Bring in a goat, and pretty soon you have a fence. Pretty soon you have a settlement. Nobody noticed. So, just do it piece by piece, and meanwhile, don't say what you're doing. That's been very effective. It's still going on.

SUREN: But doesn't that sound like a conspiratorial kind of narrative that plays into other narratives?

NOAM: It's not conspiratorial because everybody knew it. In fact, it even had slogans. This is the way to build things, step by step. Just take over a little more, take over a little more. Pretty soon, you'll have what you want. And it was a mixture of idealism, of, "We're saving the Jewish population in Eastern Europe, which is under threat and going to disappear." There were elements that said, "Look, we have to work together with the Palestinian population. We're all working people." There was an element of that. But the dominant thrust was unspoken. We were going to create the basis for a state. That certainly was the center. It wasn't formulated formally until 1942.

SUREN: And what course did people, I guess like yourself, take in response to the call for a state?

NOAM: Well, I remember in 1947 when the UN agreement was passed. It was like a day of mourning in our circles.

SUREN: But there's a deep sense of political defeat there?

NOAM: Yeah. This was the end of the hopes. And, of course, almost within days, the civil conflict developed and then blew up

PAUL: Of all your political activity ….. what was the most tense and scariest event?

NOAM: There have been tense ones. During the First Intifada in Palestine, I went with an Arab friend, and sometimes with an Israeli friend too, through villages that were under military control. In fact, we managed to break military curfew a couple of times and sometimes got caught by soldiers. Not terrifying, but you know. Again, the people are amazing. I remember going to a village that had just been virtually destroyed by an Israeli army attack. It was under military curfew. We managed to get in through the back, over the hills in the back. Half the village had been destroyed. It was probably a rainy day, and people were living out in the rain—women cooking in the rain and people huddled under blankets and so on, but they were strong. They didn't even want to talk to us until they discovered that we were not there just to watch their suffering but were concerned to help them.

CHARLIE: To follow up, you have visited the Middle East in recent years, can you describe the trip, the movements you met and the establishment responses?

NOAM: That's a long story. There were several such trips—to Gaza, Lebanon several times, Jordan (unplanned), and Palestine (blocked by Israel). I managed to reach Gaza during a period when the border to Egypt was open, joining a group of linguists from Europe and Canada who were attending an international linguistics conference at the Islamic university (soon destroyed in one of Israel's murderous assaults), all of whom also had significant activist engagement in the struggle for Palestinian rights. A very moving experience in one of the most brutalized corners of the world.

Gaza port October 20, 2012. Noam Chomsky speaks during a rally to support the Freedom Flotilla. A ship named Estelle was carrying Palestinian rights activists seeking to breach the Israeli naval blockade of Gaza.
Photo by Mahmud Hams/AFP via Getty Images

Trips to Lebanon, also between Israeli attacks, were a similar mixture of public talks, university events, interviews, meetings with activist groups, and a range of leading figures (Hassan Nasrallah, Walid Jumblatt, Sheikh Fadlallah—the target of a CIA-run terrorist bombing that missed him but killed some 80 civilians, mostly women and girls leaving a mosque). My companions and I also visited parts of the country, including the miserable camps of Palestinian refugees and the areas in the south that have been repeatedly destroyed by Israeli aggression and painstakingly rebuilt.

Khiam Prison, Lebanon, May 13, 2006. Chomsky speaks to Hezbollah leader Sheikh Nabil Qaouq and professor Fawaz Trabelsi at the former Israeli jail in southern Lebanon.
Photo by Mahmoud Zayat/AFP via Getty Images.

My aborted visit to Palestine was at the invitation of the major West Bank university, Bir Zeit. My daughter Aviva and I were detained at the Jordan-Palestine border by the ruling Israeli authorities, interrogated for several hours, then barred entry and returned to Jordan—where I was able to give the planned talk at Bir Zeit thanks to Al-Jazeera, reaching a far greater audience than had I been admitted to the occupied West Bank. When it became something of an international incident, Israel concocted a tale about a border guard who made a mistake. In fact, the interrogator was on the phone constantly with officials in Tel Aviv who were feeding him questions, keeping to the standard format—lots of irrelevant questions and then regularly the one that concerns them, in this case: why AREN'T you visiting Israel? If I'd agreed to go to Israel I would have been admitted, and could then have gone to Bir Zeit as I'd done before, from Israel. But evidently the Israeli authorities didn't want Palestine's major university to be able to invite lecturers from abroad on its own.

There's a lot more to say about all of these visits.

PAUL: Of all the things that you've done, what period or what events did you find the most hopeful? One that really just made you feel things could change, [that] we're getting somewhere?

NOAM: Well, the most hopeful, actually, are involvement with the really poor and deprived people who were struggling and achieving. I visited an extremely poor village in Southern Colombia that was miles from the nearest road—only could get to it through an almost impassable dirt road. On the way, there's a small graveyard with crosses where people were murdered by paramilitaries. In the village themselves, very friendly, warm, inviting you in. They were struggling against an effort by miners to destroy what would amount to their water supply. Watching people like that, they actually did something. The reason I went was because I had been in southern Colombia a number of times to the conflicted areas.

My late wife died 10 years ago. They were setting up a memorial for her on the top of the nearby mountain. We all climbed up the mountain. There were shamans, and they had a ceremony, and put up a plaque. It was part of their effort to protect the virgin forest and the mountain and the water supply from miners. The first time I was supposed to go, we couldn't go because there was too much violence in the area. Then, there happened to be a period of quiet. These people are really dedicated. The kind of human sympathy that you just don't see in many places. That's the kind of thing that's inspiring.

I've seen that all over the world.

PAUL: They had a memorial for your wife?

NOAM: Yeah.

PAUL: Wow.

NOAM: I had a horrible experience of riding a horse up the hill. That was the scariest thing I ever did.... They got the oldest, quietest nag in the village and put me on top of it, but I was so terrified, I couldn't even hold the reins. I just held the saddle.

PAUL: That was scarier than riding your bike on the Great Wall of China?

NOAM: Yeah.

You see examples of remarkable bravery, like in Turkey once, in southeastern Turkey, Kurdish areas where the Turks in the 1990s were carrying out really horrible atrocities against the Kurdish population. I was there, and I was giving a talk in Diyarbakır, Kurdish capital in southeast Turkey. Right after the talk, a couple young boys came up to the front and handed me a book, which I have. It was a Kurdish-Turkish dictionary. Kurdish language was outlawed. If you even pretended it existed, you could get sent to a Turkish jail. Not a nice place, if you even survive. There were Turkish security officers all over. There were television people that came up and gave me the book. They were immediately arrested. You see things like that all over the world. In the south, too.

Another moving experience I've had was in Jackson, Mississippi, at a demonstration, which was pretty bloody and brutal. In the evening, people gathered in a black church and sang hymns and so on. Sort of developed the community spirit which said okay, we'll go out again tomorrow. Those things are really gripping.

CHARLIE: Another trip that must have been very interesting would have been your Australian visits— including the reception of the Sydney Peace Prize. Can you describe the debates that surrounded the award? What about earlier trips, especially given Australia's role in East Timor and Indonesia?

NOAM: My first visit to Australia was at the invitation of my friend José Ramos-Horta, the leading out-of-country representative of the resistance to the US-backed Indonesian invasion, which came as close to true genocide as anything in the post-World War II era; he later was elected president of independent Timor l'Este (East Timor), which miraculously survived the assault. Ramos-Horta was speaking for the East Timor Refugee Association (ETRA), the organization of the many Timorese who fled the atrocities and were supported by a wonderful array of Australian activists. ETRA organized events in Sydney and Melbourne, with cultural and political programs and talks (including mine). They also arranged a press conference and other events for me in the capital, Canberra. The Australian media are a mixed story, but they were far and away the best source for the shocking events in East Timor, quite effectively suppressed in the

US, including the crucial US role from the first days. In this case too amnesia reigns. Thus in Samantha Power's much-lauded denunciation of the US for failing to respond properly to the crimes of others, she does mention East Timor, where the US regrettably "looked away," she reports—in fact, the US looked right there, closely, from the first moment, providing a "green light" for the invasion as well as arms for the assault. Power's distinguished predecessor as UN Ambassador, Daniel Patrick Moynihan, proudly took credit in his memoirs for blocking any UN reaction to the massacres.

On the later visit in which I received the Peace award—presented, I was very pleased to discover, by a leading indigenous activist—I also was able to meet with activists (including by then close friends) and give talks in several cities, and to participate in peace and justice events at schools and elsewhere.

The Case of Brazil

Background: In August 2016, the Brazilian federal legislature ousted the country's first female president, Dilma Rousseff, a former guerilla and leader of the Workers Party, in what was widely seen as a "soft" coup. By 2018, her predecessor and the leading candidate in that year's presidential election, Luis Inácio Lula da Silva (Lula), was jailed while appealing corruption convictions. Strangely, Lula himself was never shown to be the beneficiary of any alleged corrupt acts. In fact, his conviction and imprisonment are now viewed to be examples of "lawfare" wherein legal proceedings are used to undermine the public will. Recordings and text messages subsequently revealed a close, secret collaboration between the prosecutors and judge in charging Lula. Soon after his imprisonment, Noam and Valeria Chomsky traveled to Brazil where they met with the then jailed Lula. The visit made international and national headlines and seemed to channel global outrage at Lula's imprisonment. Noam Chomsky held several press conferences, wrote op-eds, and met with Workers Party activists about Lula's unjust incarceration. In those activities, he helped shape public opinion by calling attention not only to the growing rightwing threat to Brazilian democracy, but also the parallel activities by international capital. By financializing Brazil's assets and divesting from its productive base, finance capital encouraged the export of raw materials derived from extractive enterprises especially mining and forestry, all deeply implicated in environmental destruction and climate change. Significantly, activists have used Noam's analysis and commentary in their framing of the large-scale fires that scarred the Amazon in 2019.

CHARLIE: You have visited many parts of the world, often as guests of social movements, often also to the consternation of governments the local ruling classes. Taking Brazil for example, in stark contrast to your reception in 2003 when Lula was just elected, in 2018 you visited Lula in jail on the eve of an election that he most likely would have won. In his place, however, we have a fascist. What was your reception in Brazil? Did the national media cover your visit? What did social movements there expect of you?

NOAM: The matter is important enough to merit some more extended comment, particularly because of its import and the marginalization of the events, not unrelated. My wife Valeria and I visited Lula in prison in October 2018, during the run-up to the presidential election—which Lula almost certainly would have won; he was far ahead in polls when he was jailed, on very dubious charges, based on a plea bargain. Even if one believes the charges, they are minor in comparison to the guilt of his accusers, and so utterly disproportionate to the sentence, that there can be no doubt that he is a political prisoner.

Lula was sentenced to over 12 years, a virtual death sentence, in solitary confinement. He is denied access to anything in print—books, journals, press—even to TV, except for one (useless) channel. There are very

September 20, 2018, Curitiba, Brazil. Chomsky speaks to rally after visiting former president Luiz Inacio Lula da Silva in prison. Photo by Heuler Andrey/AFP via Getty Images.

limited visitation rights. Furthermore, he is barred from making any public statement, unlike mass murderers on death row.

It can hardly be doubted that the timing and outrageous sentence were designed to silence him completely before the election. Lula is, in fact the world's most important political prisoner, I believe. The fact that this scandal receives so little international attention tells us quite a lot about reigning ideology.

(Note: At the end of 2019, after serving 580 days in jail, Lula was released from prison pending appeals following a successful legal/political fight)

Silencing Lula is the latest stage in a right-wing coup that has been underway for several years. The first major step was the impeachment of Lula's successor, Dilma Rousseff, on derisory grounds. She was impeached by an impressive gang of thieves, most of whom merit long jail sentences. One of the delegates dedicated his vote of impeachment to the chief torturer of the vicious military government, who was responsible for Dilma's torture.

That's Jair Bolsonaro, the current president. Pretty low even by the abysmal standards of this shameful figure.

Gore Vidal once described the United States as "the United States of amnesia." The phrase applies very well to Brazil.

Alone among the countries that endured horrific US-backed military dictatorships during the plague of repression that swept the continent from the Kennedy to Reagan terms, Brazil has never faced up to what happened in those grim years. No punishment, not even a Truth Commission. The result is that especially younger people are often unaware of the horrors of the dictatorship and do not react appropriately when Bolsonaro praises the dictatorship, criticizing it only because it did not murder 30,000 people, like the Argentines.

Also largely forgotten—more accurately, carefully suppressed—is what the World Bank (May 2016) calls "the golden decade," the years of Lula's presidency, a unique period of the country's history when

Brazil's socioeconomic progress has been remarkable and internationally noted..... the country has
become recognized for its success in reducing poverty and inequality and its ability to create jobs.
Innovative and effective policies to reduce poverty and ensure the inclusion of previously excluded groups have lifted millions of people out
of poverty.

Furthermore,

Brazil has also been assuming global responsibilities. It has been successful in pursuing economic
prosperity while protecting its unique natural patri-
mony. Brazil has become one of the most important
emerging new donors, with extensive engagements
particularly in Sub-Saharan Africa, and a leading
player in international climate negotiations. Brazil's
development path over the past decade has shown
that growth with shared prosperity, but balanced
with respect for the environment, is possible. Bra-
zilians are rightly proud of these internationally
recognized achievements.

Critics claim that the social and economic success was
superficial, dependent on rise in commodity prices,
and that their decline led to the subsequent recession
that has been exploited by the rightwing coup. The
World Bank rejects this claim, with good reason,
matters I've discussed elsewhere. That aside, the same

rise in price for oil, soy, etc., did not lead to a similar "golden decade" elsewhere—in the United States, for example, with its extraordinary advantages.

The ongoing coup along with the effective suppression of the dictatorship and the achievements of the "golden decade" reflect in part the intense class hatred of Brazilian elites, who could not tolerate the idea that a working class leader who didn't even speak proper Portuguese could become not only president but perhaps the most respected figure on the world stage. Such people should be humble, relying on the largesse of their superiors. Government should be in the hands of "the better sort" of people, men of wealth and property, not workers, shopkeepers, skilled craftsmen. The country will be ruined if it falls "into the hands of those whose ability or situation in life does not entitle them to it," to men of "stupidity, vice, meanness," of "indigence, ignorance and baseness."

The sentiments are those of the highly class conscious Brazilian elite, but the words are those of the Founding Fathers of the United States as they carried out "the Framers' Coup," establishing an "aristocratic" form of government in which the dangerous democratic instincts of the unworthy majority were effectively tamed. The phrase "Framers Coup" is the title of the leading scholarly study of the making of the US Constitution (by Michael Klarman).

The attitudes of the self-described "men of best quality" during the English revolution of the 1640s were similar, and in fact are echoed through history whenever "the rabble" forget their proper place as subjects. Brazil today is undergoing one of those episodes—in this case threatening global survival if (president) Bolsonaro makes good on his announced plans to open the Amazon, the world's greatest carbon sink, to further exploitation by the mining and agribusiness interests that sponsored him.

Fifteen thousand people packed Gigantinho Stadium in Porto Alegre to hear Noam Chomsky and Arundhati Roy speak at the World Social Forum, January 27, 2003, soon after Lula assumed office earlier that month. View from the stage where Chomsky is speaking.
Photo by Andre Felipe/Getty Images.

Turning finally to your question, I arrived to take part in an international conference on "Threats to Democracy and Multipolar Order," with no specific reference to Brazil though the subtext—the ongoing rightwing coup—was clear enough. Participants included former prime ministers of France and Spain, the elected president of Mexico in 1988 (Cuauhtémoc Cárdenas; that election was stolen from him), prominent scholars and others from Brazil. There was not a word about the conference in the media. That's not unusual. To take a more dramatic example, shortly after, the world press reported the enormous women's demonstrations throughout the country protesting Bolsonaro's candidacy. The Brazilian media were apparently silent, apart from one photo of the huge crowd. The crucial double amnesia I mentioned earlier is also a contribution of the mass media. But the most insidious media role was in the social media, the apps on which most of the population rely, which were flooded with grotesque demonization of Lula's Workers Party (PT) and glorification of Bolsonaro, probably with initiatives tracing back to the United States, though it is not certain.

Social movements were quite different. Valeria and I met with popular groups and activists, had many interviews and discussions, and were able to meet the two most credible candidates, Ciro Gomes and Fernando Haddad (who replaced Lula on the PT ticket), both impressive figures.

Part 2

Movements Matter

The Democrats (who are not "the left" by any means) essentially abandoned the working class by the 1970s, and that continues to the present. Thus Democrats were greatly cheered by their perceived success in the 2018 mid-term elections, when they were able to flip affluent suburban voters who are disgusted by Trump's antics—while again abandoning working people to their bitter class enemy. There have been moments when white working class voters thought that the Democrats might represent their interests. Many voted for Obama in 2008, believing his message of "hope" and "change," but were quickly disillusioned, realizing that they had once again been abandoned. In the regressive US political system, it is not easy for a third party to participate in electoral politics, but there are ways through fusion candidates and the like. And it may be possible for left activists to shift the Democratic Party in more social democratic directions, responding authentically to the very real and pressing needs of the majority of the population who have been victims of the neoliberal policies of the past generation. These policies have sharply concentrated wealth while real wages have stagnated or worse, and benefits have declined along with the "growing worker insecurity" hailed by Fed chair Alan Greenspan when he was explaining to Congress the achievements of the great economy he was administering in the Clinton years. The remarkable success of the Sanders campaign, breaking with over a century of history of mostly bought elections, is an indication of what can be done, and is in part being done with the election of young progressive candidates.

But for the left, the electoral system, while of significance, is a side concern. Its real continuing task is to foster the development of popular grass-roots movements, and crucially, to help revitalize the labor movement, bringing in the alienated and disillusioned workers. These workers have been abandoned during the years of neoliberal globalization and harsh attacks on labor from the bitterly anti-labor Reagan administration and on to the present escalating class war targeting workers' rights—even the right to receive one's paycheck. Expediting the enormous crimes of wage theft is one of the priorities of the major corporate lobby ALEC (American Legislative Exchange Council), devoted to stealth subversion of democracy and elementary human rights. These powerful assaults on elementary rights, ranging very widely through the domains of basic human concerns (education, health, employment, and more) have to be exposed and countered by militant popular action, perhaps linked to electoral politics but not subordinated to the political process.

3   Coming Together

Organizing for Survival with Justice

Noam Chomsky, Charles Derber, Suren Moodliar, and Paul Shannon

SUREN: One sort of big-picture framing question. A few years back a friend noted that he is really optimistic about the future of social movements. Not so much, however, about humanity's. Do you think there's ever been a period in our history where significant numbers of people have felt that way?

NOAM: Well, there certainly have been darker moments than this. My childhood, for example, was a much grimmer period than now. But there was optimism about social movements in the 1930s. There was CIO organizing, pressures to develop the New Deal measures. A general feeling of hopefulness.

In fact, it's kind of interesting to compare the period then with the period today. Most of my extended family was working class, first-generation immigrants. Mostly unemployed... but there was a feeling of hopefulness.

First of all, they were engaged. They had a lively social and cultural life, mostly around the labor unions, which were a center of cultural activity, free time, other activities. And a sense that, "Somehow, we'll get out of this."

On the other hand, if you took a look at Europe at the same time, this really grim shadow of fascism expanding over the whole continent and going who knew how far? And with plenty of resonance here in the United States. That looked extremely frightening. So, you had a combination of concern about the future of the world, and we're Jewish, so special concern there, for obvious reasons. At the same time, a sense of local optimism for things we could do right here.

Whereas, today, there's striking sense of hopelessness, that we're lost. "Nothing can be done." A large part of it, I think, has to do with the fact that the labor movement has been pretty much subdued, if not crushed, whereas then, it was lively, exciting, developing, the forefront of everything that was happening, and the centerpiece of people's lives. For working people.

SUREN: So, the destruction of the labor unions especially in the 1980s was critical. Prior to that, there was its special construction in a pro-business direction. But, since the destruction of the labor movement, one of the things I've heard from you often is almost a celebration of the fact that there are so many different forms of resistance flourishing often in unexpected places. And yet, there seems to be a lack of coordination, the absence of a mechanism to bring people back together and to focus on achieving great common objectives. How would you compare, say, the moment of the 1930s and '40s and senses of hope, versus the current period where we don't have a powerful labor movement, but we have all these other diverse forms of resistance...

NOAM: If you look over a little broader sweep of American history and especially the 1920s, the labor movement had been crushed by violence. It had been a pretty lively, vibrant labor movement, but it really had been almost crushed. The great labor historian David Montgomery has a book called *The Fall of the House of Labor*. It's about the 1920s. So, it was resurrected from ashes, which I think that could happen again. Different circumstances, different kind of labor movement. That was a movement based on industrial installations, where large numbers of workers were together. Now we have a different kind of labor movement. Service workers, temporary workers, it's scattered. But there are things that can be done. But it's true that there are lots of activism today; if you just count the number of people involved, it is probably about as high as it's ever been. Higher than the 1950s, much higher. But it is atomized, as a reflection of the fact that the society is atomized. People are separated from one another.

4 Enhanced Exploitation

The Neoliberal Project

Noam Chomsky, Charles Derber,
Suren Moodliar, and Paul Shannon

CHARLIE: You have been writing a great deal about neo-liberalism. How do activists counter it?

NOAM: There are many counter forces. Let's go back to the United States. The situation for organizing here is not that bleak. If you take a look at the election in 2016, Clinton won a majority of the votes so other things explain Trump's victory having to do with special features of the US electoral system, which is pretty regressive by world standards. Among younger people, Clinton did win a substantial majority. More important, Sanders won an overwhelming majority. That's the younger part of the population. You take a look at Trump supporters. Many of them voted for Obama. They were seduced by this slogan which was Hope and Change. They pretty quickly find out they're not getting hope and they're not getting change. In 2016, they voted for someone else that's going for hope and change, different orientation (Trump). They want change. They're right. The situation that much of the work force and lower middle class has lived in is, it's not starvation but it's stagnation.

Just to illustrate, in 2007, which is the peak of what was hailed then as an economic miracle right before the crash, working people, non-supervisory workers, their real wages were lower, considerably lower than they had been in 1979. Just when the neoliberal onslaught was beginning. The minimum wage, which had been tracking productivity, flattened. Meaning, lower than it should be. If it had continued the way it did during the big growth period, it would probably be something like $20 an hour now. It's now considered revolutionary to call for $15 an hour. The minimum wage is a base for the wages. It's an indication of what much of the population recognizes to be stagnation or decline.

Meanwhile, the neoliberal projects, including the global ones, have been designed to set working people into competition with one another all over the world while protecting professional elites. Philippine doctors can't practice. Professional elites are protected. Of course, the so-called trade agreements are really basically investor rights agreements. Not much to do with trade but have plenty to do with protecting the mega-corporations, like pharmaceuticals. Just the increase in prices due to the protectionist elements of the trade agreements is an enormous tax burden for the general public. It drives prices of drugs way beyond what they would be in any market system.

This is across the board. Won't go through the details. A system has been designed. It's not economic laws. It's policy and decisions, which has been quite harmful to a large mass of the population. In fact a majority. It's also undermined democracy, both here and even more so in Europe. There's a natural and justified call for change. These are opportunities for the left. Many of the people who voted for Trump could have voted for Bernie Sanders.

5 Identity Politics and Class Politics

Common Interests, Labor, and Collective Action

Noam Chomsky, Charles Derber,
Suren Moodliar, and Paul Shannon

CHARLIE: Some argue that the left has crafted an identity politics to focus on race, gender and ethnicity without any attention to the larger economic and political forces that you just described. Do you share that feeling, that the Democratic Party and the Left itself bear responsibility for abandoning class politics and for a siloed identity politics? It's speaking to coastal elites, it's speaking to educated people, speaking to young educated people. It's not speaking to working class people of all races and genders hit hard by neoliberalism and class exploitation.

NOAM: Not speaking to people who are really deprived.

It should be working with the African American community, it should be working on civil rights, it should be working for gay rights, for women's rights, and so on. That's fine. What it has dropped pretty much is class issues. The Democratic Party just largely down-played these issues since the beginning of the Clinton era.

CHARLIE: Do you see class politics as a priority for the left in the next, immediate period of time? Do you see... a Sanders or Warren style move-ment as a response? Not that it abandons the most depressed racial and gendered identity groups in the society, but it finds a way to deal with those forces, as you say, as integrated with the larger capitalist system.

NOAM: It's certainly a must. These so called identity politics are great successes in themselves, but when they are designed and presented in such a way that they appear to be an attack on the lifestyle, val-ues, commitments of a large part of the popula-tion, there's going to be reaction. That shouldn't be done.

CHARLIE: For example, the movement uses the lan-guage of white privilege. Some of the people from white working-class areas, they look at that and they say, "What are you talking about? We're not seeing this privilege." Does this require the left to re-assess its vocabulary?

NOAM: It's not just about our vocabulary. It's about an understanding. Actually, Arlie Hochschild's book is very revealing in this respect.

CHARLIE: Her book is called, *Strangers in Their Own Land*, a best-seller about Southern workers and Christians who supported Trump in 2016.

NOAM: Everybody knows the story. She's lived for many years in the Bayou country in Louisiana and gave a very sympathetic understanding, conception of what the people are thinking and why—from a point of view of a Berkley progressive, who she is. She was accepted into the community. It's very revealing. The images she uses, which they accepted as the correct one, is that people... They see themselves as standing in a line. They've been working hard all their lives, their parents work hard, they're doing all the right things in a conservative, religious area. They go to church, they read the Bible, they have traditional families and so on. They've done everything the right way.

All of the sudden the line is stalled. Up ahead of them, there are people leaping forward, which doesn't bother them because according to the doctrine, that's the American way. You work hard and you have merit, strange kind of merit, you get rewards. What bothers them is that the people behind them in the line, as they see it, are being pushed ahead of them by the federal government.

CHARLIE: By liberal elites and so forth.

NOAM: By liberal elites and the federal government. That they resent. The facts are different. There's no basis in fact but you can understand the basis for the perception. That can be dealt with by serious activist organizing. Many of the people she was dealing with are environmentalists but they hate the EPA. They want to destroy the Environment Protection Agency. They themselves are committed environmentalists.

The families are very interesting. Hochschild's working in an area which is sometimes called cancer alley. Everybody's dying from cancer from the chemical pollution plants. Nevertheless, they vote for a congressman who wants to dismantle the EPA entirely. There's a reason. Turns out, there's an internal rationality to this self-destructive position. Organizers and activists can go after that. The internal rationality is that what they see is some guy from the EPA wearing a suit and jacket coming down to tell them, "You can't fish in this river." Meanwhile, he does nothing about the chemical plants. Why do they want the EPA?

CHARLIE: This is a really great example to focus in on. I think what Hochschild was able to do in this book you're describing was live with these communities and gain their trust. A lot of barriers were broken down so she could get their narrative. Do you see any examples of progressive left organizing which operates out of that Hochschild narrative and finds a way to really connect with these communities in a credible way to these people?

NOAM: There's many things like that.

CHARLIE: How about some examples?

NOAM: The core of this I think, which you've mentioned several times, is revitalizing the labor movement. That's always been and will continue to be pretty much the forefront of any progressive activities, just as it has been in the past. It's been severely damaged by national policies going back to the second World War, but escalating during the Reagan and Clinton period, the neo-liberal period. It can be revitalized. These are not people living in the bayous. They're living two miles away from us. There are things being done.

CHARLIE: You think a revival of labor as a more central player in this mosaic of progressive communities…

NOAM: Let's be concrete about it. A couple of years ago in a Boston suburb, Taunton, Mass, a multinational decided to close down a factory. It was a factory producing specialized parts for airplanes. The factory was reasonably profitable but it wasn't making enough profit for the bankers that run the multinational so they decided to close it down. The union and the workforce offered to buy it and run it themselves. It could have been run and been profitable. If they had had popular support,

community support, activist support, they could
have worked that out.

CHARLIE: That's been done. Economist Gar Alperovitz has documented that worker cooperatives are
being organized in Ohio and other parts of the
Midwest suffering deindustrialization.

NOAM: It's done, but this is a case right here in Boston. The things that Gar Alperovitz is doing in
Midwestern factories and communities, are indications of what could be done around the country.
It could be done right here. It could be done in a
mass scale. Go back to the 2008 financial crisis,
really the housing crisis which began the financial
crisis. At one point, the government, federal government, had basically nationalized the auto industry. Almost. There were choices at that point.
If there had been a left functioning it could have
influenced those choices. There was none so it
didn't influence them.

CHARLIE: You mean by a left functioning, do you
mean a more active labor, popular community
movement?

NOAM: Popular activist movements. There were
choices that could be made. One choice, the one
that was taken, was to pay off the owners and
managers, reconstitute the industry and hand it
back to the former owners or other people much

like them and have it go back to its old activities. That's the course that was taken. An alternative course would have been to have handed the industry over to the stakeholders. The work force and the community. They'd need some support but no more than... probably less than what was paid off to the companies. Instead of having them produce cars, have them own and run and manage it and produce what the country needs, which is not more cars. Drive through Boston and you see that's not what the country needs.

What we need is some reasonable system of mass transportation, which goes right to the environmental problem and many others. Even just the simple comfort of not sitting in a traffic jam all day in getting where you want to go. That would have been an alternative. Was it feasible? It would have been feasible if there were an organized activist left, just as in the Taunton case nearby. Those are directions in which activism can go. They can have massive effect on the economy, on the society, on the nature of the workforce, on what they perceive as real hope and change. Things like that can happen almost every day.

For example, take the people that Hochschild was studying on the bayou who are environmentalists, committed environmentalists, no reason why they can't work together with environmentalists who say,

"Look, let's get regulations that really work. Not just against your fishing but against your chemical companies." That's a common basis. It happens that many of them regard the Bible as a much more authentic source of information than science, but that's not graven in stone either. That can be changed.

6 Activists and Evangelicals

Organizing across the Cultural Divide

*Noam Chomsky, Charles Derber,
Suren Moodliar, and Paul Shannon*

NOAM: In the evangelical community, there have
been very progressive elements. Take the Central
America solidarity movements. They were very
significant. This is probably the first time in history that the aggressor and the country that was
responsible for the atrocities, individuals were going to help the victims. I don't think that's ever
happened before. Nobody ever dreamt of going to
a Vietnamese village to live with the villagers, to
help them to provide a white face which is a little
protection. It just never occurred to anyone. This
happened with tens of thousands of people during
the Central America solidarity period. Many of
them were evangelical.

I remember talking in evangelical churches in the
Mid-west where people not only had direct experience but also knew more about what was going on
than academics did. They were directly involved. Furthermore, after the election in Nicaragua, the right-
wing election, many of them stayed. The other ones

have stayed. There's plenty of opportunities. There's no point predicting what might happen. What you do is pursue the options and see how far they can go.

CHARLIE: The environmental movements are huge on campuses and across the country. What is your vision of how these movements could connect with these people that sociologist Arlie Hochschild was dealing with who are evangelical, who are conservative culturally?

NOAM: Organize in churches, organize in communities. How did the Central America solidarity movements develop? People totally secular and left like me were perfectly capable of working together with evangelical Christians on concrete things, like helping communities protect themselves from criminal atrocities, state crimes and so on.

CHARLIE: This would partly mean hooking up with people say like Jim Wallis, a progressive evangelical leader who is organizing young evangelicals to do that. I went South as a northern student in the 1960s and worked with the civil rights movements. Are you imagining that there might be environmentalists who are now in colleges in the north but then would go back to their native south and would work in that area?

NOAM: Civil rights movements is a good example. There was real interaction, very constructive interaction between northern college students and deeply impoverished repressed black areas in rural south. Helped each other, worked together, created bonds.

CHARLIE: I experienced that. It was powerful. I slept on the floor of a black family and lived in Jackson, Mississippi. You're saying, that's in a way a metaphor for Left organizing with Southern evangelicals or conservative workers in the Rust Belt.

NOAM: It can be done. There's no point arguing that it can't be done because the cultural differences are too great. Press forward as far as you can. My guess is one will find that the cultural differences, though they'll remain, why shouldn't they, can be overcome by common concerns and interests.

CHARLIE: So cultural conservatism and religiosity, which is very powerful in parts of the US, is real but can be overcome by progressive activists fighting for common interests?

NOAM: The cultural issue has to do with a historical phenomenon that we can't overlook. Before the second World War, the United States was of course by far the richest country in the world but it wasn't in the lead in global management. That was Britain, even France. It was a cultural backwater. I got to see this myself when I started teaching at MIT. Interesting way. MIT had courses for students who want to get a PhD. You had to pass a

reading exam in French and German which I was
teaching for a while.

Why? Because before World War II, if you wanted to
be a scientist and engineer, you had to know French
and German. That, after World War II, changed. If
you're European, you have to know English. For part
of the population, for a large part of the population,
they remained traditional, conservative, pre-modern,
subject to the Protestant reformation, Calvinist doctrine that the Bible is the truth and science doesn't
matter. The world has changed. Parts of the American
population have changed. The rest of it can change
too. It's not graven in stone. But that requires work.

CHARLIE: I think what you're saying is, contrary to
journalist Thomas Frank for example, that one can
bridge a lot of these cultural differences. You don't
want to go around labeling or dismissing these
people as cultural backwater.

NOAM: No, you don't.

CHARLIE: You want to say there are shared concerns
and vital common interests here...

NOAM: You don't come to people and say, "You're a
cultural backwater." You deal with the fact that
the beliefs that they have ought to be changed
through their own recognition that these beliefs
are not...

CHARLIE: You don't mean their cultural, values in terms of religion…

NOAM: Yes, I do.

CHARLIE: You do?

NOAM: The belief if the Bible and science conflict, science is automatically wrong, people can come to see that that's not true. Many people have. Much of the population has already passed through that change. Others can as well.

CHARLIE: That seems like a struggle because when you get to people whose lives are deeply involved with the church and Biblical studies, the beliefs are deeply entrenched. But it's true that Europe and the US are becoming more secular, perhaps related to growing education.

NOAM: It's all of us, if we go back a couple generations, that's… If I go back to my grandfather, that was his belief. Things change.

CHARLIE: That's an optimistic flavor in the analysis because you're saying the progressive community should not be deterred from seeking common ground and activism alongside cultural conservatives.

NOAM: No. It should not be deterred and it shouldn't be contemptuous. It should be sympathetic, understanding, find common ground, things you can work on. Not put aside these questions of belief and understanding. They can be changed too.

CHARLIE: Maybe the key there is people like Wallis and other evangelical leaders, younger particularly, who are politically changing. Religious beliefs evolve. Maybe that is one of the ways in which this happens.

NOAM: There are many avenues. There is urgency. We don't have a lot of time. Specifically in the climate issue.

CHARLIE: The extinction crisis raises the stakes and changes the political landscape. Young evangelicals are increasingly becoming activists to solve the climate change crisis.

NOAM: Incidentally, just look at other possible common ground. One major area is Trump's proposal for infrastructure development. The country needs that. It's needed it all along. These are actually Obama proposals which were blocked by the Republican Congress. The Republicans were a wrecking machine: "Don't allow anything to work". One of the good things about their having control of the government is that conceivably they might actually implement the policies instead of killing them. There are possible grounds for serious organizing and activism with the Trump backers and the workforce. These are jobs for them if it's done properly.

CHARLIE: Which it's not. Economist Paul Krugman wrote in 2016 a long analysis of infrastructure talking points and ideas from Trump and conservatives, which is distressing.

NOAM: We don't know. That description is what might happen, but doesn't have to happen. Popular action could shift it in a different direction, including the Trump voters who can understand that column just as well as you and I can. This can be brought to people who can see, look, the way to do it is not by huge tax credits to private industry.

CHARLIE: That's the way that Trumpists and other conservatives are thinking about it apparently, if they think about infrastructure at all.

NOAM: The fact that they may be thinking about it that way doesn't guarantee that it's going to happen that way. That depends on the way the public responds, including the Trump voters who can see just as you and I can that that's going to be harmful to them and that it should be done through a progressive government.

CHARLIE: I want to ask one other question on unions. A lot of people at the steelworker union and other major industrial unions worked their hearts out during the 2016 election. They found—the progressive film-maker Michael Moore was writing a lot about this—they found their own members were not responding for many reasons we've been touching on. The union leadership put a tremendous amount of money and staff into the 2016 elections—and they lost a lot of their own members. What does that tell us or what should we be learning from that?

NOAM: Tells us that you work harder. This can happen right at Harvard. The Harvard Trade Union Program is trying to do this. It brings together activist labor unions, young labor union activists from all over the world, international, very constructive, do really good things and go back to their own unions. There's every reason to work with them. There's a reason after all, and they know the reason why their own workers voted for Trump, because no alternative was being presented to them. Present an alternative to them. Even Sanders didn't manage really to bridge the class issue. It should be done.

CHARLIE: Despite the urgency of our US and global crises, you've offered a very realistic but hopeful view of how to invite conversation and build connections to the whole country in a way.

NOAM: Pursue the opportunities that exist. There are many of them. We don't know how far they can reach. There's no point mourning that bad things happen. Find the things that can be done, and there are many of them. Many of them with international connections because there are similar problems. Many of them integrating people who seem to be on opposite sides of the divide but really have common interests. Those could be extricated and pursued.

7 Identity, Intersectionality, and Universalizing Resistance

Noam Chomsky, Charles Derber, Suren Moodliar, and Paul Shannon

CHARLIE: I think people would be very interested in knowing more about what you think about the whole concept of identity politics. Is there a form of it that you think is defensible and, in fact, necessary and essential? How do you see it?

NOAM: I think it's necessary and essential, but the problem is not focusing on identity politics, what's called identity politics, which means the various kinds of human and civil rights. That makes perfect sense. The problem is cutting out the issue of class politics. It's what's been omitted and marginalized—the real problem. Class and identity politics should be almost completely identified. Take, say, the union movement. By now, the union movement's about half women. Is that identity politics or labor politics? Go back to the early '70s when there was a militant labor movement developing out at Lordstown, Ohio, and the farm worker strikes and so on. A lot of it was initiated by women and Hispanics, so the identity politics and the labor and the class issues could have been very closely identified. This was kind of dropped, and it's a loss and it has to be reconstructed.

CHARLIE: The working class is increasingly people of color, it's female, and other disadvantaged identity groups which have a lot of their own movements. How do you understand why these "identity" movements, as you say, have moved away from class politics and we see a kind of weak class politics?

NOAM: There's a number of reasons. For one thing, they really are important issues, so don't want to demean the issue of, say, gay rights.

CHARLIE: Absolutely. Very important.

NOAM: Not only are they important issues, but they're the kind that concentrated economic power can easily accommodate. So the corporate world has nothing against gay rights. In fact, plenty of executives and CEOs and so on support gay rights. Pushing that issue is important, but it doesn't elicit the kind of radical resistance that you get if you try to push labor rights. There, you get into a fight. So it's kind of tempting to go in the ways that will be accommodated, which is not to say they're not important. They are.

CHARLIE: In a funny way, I suppose identity politics, like you say, is crucial, but when it gets disassociated from class politics, it ends up potentially legitimating ruling elites because what it means is you're fighting for groups to get their share of the pie within the existing system.

NOAM: Within the existing system, and you're not questioning the structure of power itself, which can accommodate elements of women's rights.

CHARLIE: What would you say to people who would argue you're privileging class over race or gender orientation.

NOAM: Not privileged.

CHARLIE: Identity politics seems to suggest the structure of power is as much organized around racial hierarchies or gender hierarchies as it is around class hierarchy.

NOAM: Therefore, let's integrate them. The point is they're not separated from one another. As I said, almost half the labor movement is women, so when you're looking at reconstituting unions, you're fighting for women's rights. Much of it is Hispanic, much of it's African American, and so on. In fact, what you want to do is break down the barriers that have prevented the labor union, say, from becoming a powerful force. You look over the history of the labor movement. The times when it really was a powerful force were when these barriers were overcome. Labor organizing was black and white workers.

CHARLIE: What would you say, Noam, are the next steps? I mean, do you feel there are steps either to be taken by unions or by various civil rights, gay, feminist movements and so forth? As you say, they've sort of drifted apart to some degree. This is just sort of an impressionistic thing, but what do you think might meld them together more? Do you see campaigns right now, issues right now, that could actually see this happen, make this happen.

NOAM: There are overwhelming issues which are common to all of them. I mean, if the sea level is going to rise by 10 meters, doesn't matter what we say about gay rights. This is a common issue. We are destroying the possibility for organized human life to persist. That's a common issue. The threat of nuclear war, which is not just North Korea but all over, now that's a common issue. The gradual takeover by the right wing of the Republican Party and their careful planning over the years to take over the lower levels of government, which means gerrymandering, districts ensuring control of the Congress, creating a background in which programs like, say, those ALEC programs I mentioned can continue. That affects everybody. It affects civil rights, human rights, gay rights, everything else. The crucial problem of stagnation of wages and income for a generation for the great majority of the population—the working population—that affects everyone, and there are reasons for it. There are sources in political decisions that have led to that.

MIT, Cambridge, September 9, 2006. Noam Chomsky with Steve Meacham and Marilyn Levin.
Photo by Roger Leisner

Again, these are common issues. It's perfectly possible, in fact appropriate, to say women should get higher wages proportional to their work and say, "Look, we want to undermine the whole system of exploitation and capitalist domination, which underlies all of it." Pursuing, say, worker-owned enterprises and cooperatives—that joins everyone together and affects everybody's rights. There's no reason for these things to be separated.

CHARLIE: You know, we do see evidence of that. For example, the climate movement that you referenced is now increasingly thought of as the environmental justice movement, which high-lights the climate effects on minorities and the poor.

NOAM: There are real issues, immediate issues, that can be focused on right at the moment. Take these chemical plant explosions in Houston (in early 2019). There's a reason for them. The Republican legislature for years has refused to permit oblig-atory safety regulations to be implemented. The EPA moved in under Scott Pruitt to block efforts in the last couple of months to impose safety re-quirements. End result, you may get something like chemical warfare, and that affects mostly dis-advantaged communities. They're the ones that live near the chemical plants. There is some dis-cussion of this around the periphery. It ought to be headlines. This Houston thing, it's as if fate presented us with a model of what's destroying the world. Here you have a city with virtually no regulations, so you have a disaster when anything comes. Here you have the center of the energy industry—which is destroying the future and the possibilities for the future—and the city being in-undated and destroyed all together. It's a perfect microcosm of what we're creating.

CHARLIE: Absolutely.

NOAM: Of course, the energy corporations know all about global warming, have been building their own facilities to protect themselves from rising sea while they claim it's not happening.

CHARLIE: How would you respond to, say, an African American who is deeply involved in fighting mass incarceration, police violence against blacks, and so forth and saying, "Yeah, I understand these connections. In fact, a lot of Black Lives Matter leaders are socialists and have been overtly so," but they also say, "Look, these larger issues you're talking about are very real. We understand that, but we're dealing with an emergency on a day-to-day basis. My son just got shot by a policeman," and so forth. It's sort of managing the levels of immediate urgency that way. How do you respond to people who are dealing with the realities of that situation?

NOAM: Well, I think they have to face the immediate realities, and they also have to recognize that, as many of them do, there's a background for these realities in structural problems of the society. Black Lives Matter has been pretty effective in even gaining public support. It has about 50% public support, which is very unusual for a dissident movement. Compare it with, say, the Antifa, which has 5% support.

CHARLIE: This relates to an issue we've talked about before, which is it seems to me that Trump got elected partly by doing what you're sort of advocating for the Left. The way I've thought about it is he built a class politics. He appealed to a lot of the white working class, which had been culturally or economically abandoned by the Democratic Party, and he built an identity politics, which was drawing on all kinds of cultural differences.

NOAM: There's some of that. His actual voting base is fairly affluent. It's above the median.

CHARLIE: It's above the median, yeah. I think it's $107,000 median family income in the Trump base.

NOAM: It's mostly petite bourgeois. There are working class elements that were drawn in exactly as you say. There were people drawn in on the basis of race, white supremacy and others, but much of it is essentially rural, which can mean industrial, moderately affluent, mostly petite bourgeois demographic base. Yes, he's managed to hold onto them to an extent, which is really shocking. I mean, by now, it's almost worship. He can do nothing wrong. In fact, the poll results are astonishing. It turns out that among Republican voters, trust in Trump is far higher than trust in, say, Fox News. I mean, if he says something is true, doesn't matter what anyone says. Of course, CNN or the NY Times, they're just nothing.

CHARLIE: What do you make of that? Why do you think this particular part of the population is so identified with him?

NOAM: Well, I think part of it may be just desperation. The whole contempt for the political system is just overwhelming. That's been true for years. Support for Congress has hovered around single digits. Similarly, in Europe, where the centrist parties are collapsing, and for good reasons. The political system is not working in the interests of the general population, and it's led to contempt and anger. Well, here's somebody who says, "Okay, I'm going to fix that." You kind of grab onto it like a drowning man grabs onto a life raft. Part of it is just that he's making it possible for sections of the population to come forward with views that they've always held but felt repressed that they shouldn't say because what's called, interestingly, political correctness, which means don't be an overt racist. Now, you can be an overt racist and it's fine, so it's gratifying. There's lots of reasons, I think, people are grasping in a kind of desperation. It's an interesting question whether it'll hold when his own voting base, say rural Arkansas, realizes that this guy is smashing you in the face every time he has a chance. Is that going to change things?

CHARLIE: Do you think that progressives, meaning the Left and parts of the Democratic Party, can reach such people? I mean, you talked about people whose subliminal or covert racism is attracting them to Trump, and you've talked about that cultural backwater of the United States, the history of the South. Do you sort of feel like we live in a country where progressives have to write off, simply because of this culture and history, a significant sector of the population if they get the great majority in their camp?

NOAM: Take a look at American history. The most radical general popular movement that ever developed in the United States began with Texas farmers. It spread through Kansas.

CHARLIE: Kansas, yeah. The 19th century populists.

NOAM: The agrarian populist movement was extremely radical. It was ultimately crushed, but those people are still there.

CHARLIE: So your view is that the country remains receptive to a transformative vision. Because the system is failing people, there's actually an opportunity now for the Left to grow.

NOAM: To say, "Look, here's something real, not a con." If you can come to people and say, "Look, here's something real that'll affect you and your lives, your children's lives, the future," that can attract people.

CHARLIE: Give me, again, more concrete examples of what's working best right now or might work best?

NOAM: Houston, since it happens to be in the front pages (2019). Say, look, what's happening in

Houston? The failure of a regulatory apparatus has created the basis for a disaster of which the perpetrators will benefit, because they'll be bailed out. Oil prices will go up, so they'll be rich, and so on. It's also creating a situation in which your children are not going to be able to survive, and it's affecting you directly, because of the toxins from these chemical plants, which are pouring out because the legislators that you voted for refuse to impose safety regulations. Why are they doing it? Because the way the country works is the political system responds to the wealthy, not to you. All of this ties together, beginning with the fact that your kids may get cancer and that you're under water.

CHARLIE: We're not seeing this in Texas. I saw an interview with a guy who is heading a Texan secession movement whose house got flooded. He doesn't want to have anything to do with the federal government, but he now supports the federal government because he says, well, there are few legitimate federal functions, one of which is fund relief at some point.

NOAM: Funding me.

CHARLIE: Yeah, funding me. But the situation you're describing in Texas has not produced a progressive outpouring.

NOAM: But it can. It provides an opening for forces to provide what is not being provided. You're right, it's not producing that, but that's the failure of the Left to provide that.

CHARLIE: But you do see opportunities that progressives are beginning to seize?

NOAM: There is plenty of organizing and activism on these things, just not enough. I picked Houston only because it's on the front pages. We could pick anything else. A war with, a blow-up with Iran, is going to affect everyone.

CHARLIE: What about DACA? We're talking on a morning when Trump is going to revoke DACA. What is the progressive activist response to that?

NOAM: It's kind of interesting, but the progressive response is pretty much that of the business community. Different reasons, but the same conclusion. The reason should be these people have a right to stay here. The business world says we need them, but they happen to be converging on the same conclusion, so fine. That's a large part of the country agrees with that, probably a large majority.

CHARLIE: I guess one of the reasons to be hopeful is that public opinion polls support your view. On issue after issue, people tend to be left of center. Anti big corporations. Pro unions. More publicly funded education and health care. Less big money in politics. Increasingly even favorable to the word "socialism."

NOAM: Take healthcare. The population for years has been receptive or sometimes supportive of the kind of healthcare system that other developed societies have, which is not particularly utopian. Can do much better than that, in fact, but at least as good as other developed societies have instead of the scandal we have. Population is receptive, sometimes supportive of that, and organizing can be done around that. That's an immediate concern for people.

CHARLIE: Absolutely.

NOAM: That's immediate—can I go to a doctor tomorrow.

CHARLIE: There are a lot of scary things happening in the world, What is your sense? Do you feel, personally, optimistic that the Left and progressive forces can grow and ultimately save society, or are we sort of in a quagmire in which the right wing has so much money and so much political power and so much gerrymandered force and so on that we're in a very dicey situation?

NOAM: I think we're in a dicey situation, but there are many opportunities. How it'll play out depends on the choices that people make. How much do you become engaged in exploiting the opportunities that are available to push forward on many fronts, from the personal and individual up to the societal and international. They're all tied together, and we have many ways of acting. We've talked about a handful of them. We can go on. These are things that can be pursued. Can they be won? We don't know. If you extrapolate from what's now happening, we'll probably be under water in a couple of generations. Just take a look at the long-term history. About 120,000 years ago, the Earth's temperature was a little bit above what it is now. Not massively above. We're getting there. The sea level was about 30 yards higher. What happens to most of the world now? That's the trajectory we're on. Doesn't have to be. There are ways out.

8   Activism and Fascism
Then and Now

Noam Chomsky, Charles Derber,
Suren Moodliar, and Paul Shannon

CHARLIE: Right wing and fascist movements succeeded partly because they appealed to the irrational. The Frankfurt School of German intellectuals after World War II highlighted Hitler's success in appealing to emotions such as fear and authoritarianism. Does the Left need to appeal to emotions and the irrational as well, rather than only focusing on rationality and rational self-interest? If so, what emotions can it tap into?

NOAM: It has often been argued that because of "the stupidity of the average man," it is necessary to provide the lesser orders with "emotionally potent simplifications" and "necessary illusions" to guide them in the right direction (Reinhold Niebuhr, expressing views that are quite common among liberal intellectuals). One can understand why such ideas should appeal to a potential leadership class, to those who regard themselves as "the better sort of men," in the words of the Founding Fathers. Putting aside the validity of the argument—or to be more accurate, the declaration, since there is no argument—history gives us ample evidence of where that leads, just as should be anticipated. I think we would do better to harken to the words of Rosa Luxemburg in her critique of the Leninist version of such conceptions, and place our hopes more in the "great creative acts of the often spontaneous class struggle seeking its way forward." No room for romanticism about folk wisdom, but plenty of room, I think, for sympathy for Jefferson's disdain (in words at least) for the "aristocrats" who seek to arrogate power and decision-making to themselves—and his preference for democrats who identify with and have confidence in the people, and consider them the most "honest & safe," even if not always wise, "depository of the public interest."

SUREN: In the 1930s, fascism was ascendant in Europe. Today, we have a second act. But in no way does it seem identical to what happened in the 1930s. There doesn't seem to be a mass movement, as such.

NOAM: Well, don't forget, in the 1930s, first of all, by the 1930s, fascism had been established in Italy for 15 years. It was running the place. Nazism was taking over by 1934, 1935. They were taking over Germany, which is the center of Europe. They were quite strong in France. Austria was incorporated in 1938. The Spanish war '36 to '39. It was moving towards a fascist victory. It just looked like it was going everywhere. I've heard this before, but the first article that I remember writing in 1939 on the fall of Barcelona was mainly about the sense that fascism was just going to spread everywhere. And it was pretty grim. I mean, there are neo-fascist movements, but they are not running the world and carrying out massive atrocities and so on. It was already going on then.

"They shall not pass!" banner in Madrid, 1936 or 1937, during the Spanish Civil War.
Photo by Mikhail Koltsov/Wikimedia Commons.

They were also being tolerated by the West. It's called appeasement, but that is misleading. British business had pretty good relations with German fascism. In the United States, the State Department was urging tolerance for not only fascism, which was admired—Italian fascism was admired openly—but even Nazism. In fact, the United States had a Consul in Berlin up until Pearl Harbor. The head of the Consul was writing back pretty positive messages, saying "You have a lot of things we don't like about Nazism, but there are some good things about it." He was not an obscure figure. That's George Kennan, who's considered one of the great statesmen of the 20th century, which indicates what attitudes were like. I mean, "The Nazis are not all bad. They're smashing the labor movement, they're barring Bolshevism, the great threat since 1917. So, we can kind of work with them."

Mussolini was openly admired. I mean, in almost a racist fashion. So, Fortune magazine, the main business magazine in, I think, 1932 or so. (Keep in mind that Fascism had been in place for almost a decade.) They had a major issue, in which the headline was, "The wops are unwopping themselves." The Italians are finally getting it together. The motto was, "The trains are running on time." They're doing things right. None of this radicalism that we're scared of.

The Bolshevik revolution had a huge impact on American elites. They were terrified. That led to the Red Scare, which was the worst repression in American history, by liberals, incidentally. It went on like that. So, the fascists were kind of tolerated. Hitler could have been stopped in 1935 or 1936, maybe later.

SUREN: With that in mind, how do you approach our current responses, both as, I guess, on the one end, the more liberal establishment left, and then the far left? Although I wouldn't want to establish any kind of symmetry between the far left and the far right. They're very different.

NOAM: There's no symmetry. There are small elements of the far left which I think are following self-destructive tactics. Unprincipled and self-destructive, and they're causing problems for themselves and everyone else. In fact, they're already on the terrorist lists. Pretty soon it'll be expanded. That could lead to much wider repression. It's an adventurist and thoughtless reaction, and also achieving nothing. But it's there. That's extremely unpopular, in fact. If you look at the polls, the alt-right has almost no support. It's maybe 5%. Antifa has about the same support. In contrast, Black Lives Matter has about 50% support, even though many people find it very provocative. There's a lot of public support.

There are methods that can be used that are effective. We saw this in the Civil Rights Movement. I mean, the SNCC (Student Non-violent Coordinating Committee) workers in the South who took the N in their name pretty seriously, the non-violent part. They were facing violence of a kind that nobody's facing today. Freedom riders were getting murdered, beaten. The black farmers that were joining them, it was even worse. The violence was much more extreme than today, but it was... It's not that people didn't defend themselves, that's okay, but it was basically a non-violent appeal, which turned out to be extremely effective. That's not the only case. There are studies which show pretty conclusively that non-violent movements and programs are far more successful. Once you move into the arena of violence, the tougher and more brutal guys win. That's not us.

SUREN: If we ought to provide some positive encouragement to people on the left who are distressed that the far right is able to march, to take advantages of the opportunities that Trump and all present, what kind of advice would we want to give them?

NOAM: I would say, first of all, they're a small group. The advice is, "Let them march, but you march 100 times as much and expose what they're doing." Exposure is the best remedy. Let them expose themselves as neo-Nazis and racists. They'll elicit a huge counter-response, and they'll fade away. That's pretty much what happened in Boston. What happened in Skokie, Illinois, which was very provocative. An openly neo-Nazi group wanted to march through a Jewish area with lots of Holocaust victims, with Nazi slogans. "Kill the Jews," and so on. They were defended by the ACLU, correctly, I think. There was public organization to protest the march non-violently, that they just didn't go. They disappeared and, in fact, the group disappeared. That's the right way to respond.

SUREN: How do we coordinate our response to the urgency of counteracting the far-right via large marches and more effective, more organized forces?

NOAM: Not just by large marches, by using the opportunity. I mean, take this business with statues. The right reaction, I think, is one that was tried and didn't succeed because it didn't have enough support at Stanford University. Stanford University is named after Leland Stanford, a guy who made his fortune by vicious exploitation of Chinese workers who were kidnapped from China and built the railroads. There's a big statue of him in Stanford, naturally. So, the students suggested, not taking the statue away, but putting next to it a statue of a Chinese coolie and using that as an opportunity for education about what we're about and how we got there. That would have been the right thing to do. The elites understood that, so they went all out preventing it, not that it would have been easier to take the statue away than to put this counter-statue. And that tells you what's the right thing to do.

SUREN: Governor Baker in Massachusetts is very ready to talk about moving particular monuments and that kind of thing, but definitely not to engage in the counter-statue movement.

NOAM: Well, I think that's the part that's really frightening to elite power, and that means that's what you should be doing.

SUREN: So, that would potentially open up lots of conversations about what actually happened in that period, that kind of thing.

NOAM: So, next to Robert E. Lee, put statues and memorials indicating what was the nature of African slavery here. It was the worst, most vicious slavery in the history of the world, and that should be exposed. Not by taking away a statue but by teaching people about it. Because, if you take away the statue, the residue is still there. It's there in the prisons, for example. Why do you have this prison? It's a residue of slavery. So, let's teach that, not take the statue away, but teach that.

SUREN: So, more speech. Not less speech.

NOAM: Yes, and more education and understanding. And that can be achieved. It's kind of interesting. Last Sunday, for example, take a look at the review section of the *New York Times*. They had a front page article on genocide in California, which would have just been unimaginable 10 years ago, 50 years ago. Nobody even knew what you were talking about. Now, it's the front page of the *New York Times* pulling that with no stops, telling the story very straight. Genocide of the American Native population. Okay, that's real change.

Just to give you one more example, I think it's Los Angeles, some big city just changed Columbus Day to Indigenous American Day. Okay, that's a portent.

CHARLIE: Is Trump a neo-fascist? Do you agree with Leftists who believe it is accurate to view Trump through the lens of fascism? Or does the Trump phenomenon fit into a different political framing.

NOAM: The word "fascist" has become pretty much a term of abuse. If we have in mind the fascist movements of earlier years, I don't think the term applies to Trump. He is not seeking to construct a powerful state that will control and integrate the centers of private power and dominate all sectors of social and cultural life. On the contrary, he is the faithful servant of private wealth and corporate power. His main (in fact sole) legislative triumph, the tax scam of 2017, is a clear illustration. His ideology seems to reduce to the simple principle: ME! His narcissistic megalomania has several corollaries. To maintain power, he has to serve the interests of his primary constituency, private wealth and corporate power. And he must somehow maintain his voting base: mainly the affluent, but in addition evangelical Christians, disillusioned workers, white supremacists and in general those whose pathological instincts he very effectively fosters. He's been a brilliant success so far in serving the primary constituency while maintaining the loyalty (sometimes worship) of a popular base that is being shafted at every turn by his service to the primary constituency. It's an impressive performance. But I think it is a mistake to try to concoct some socioeconomic theory behind it, just as I think it is a mistake to seek to discern some geopolitical strategy behind his various wild shots in the global system, sometimes actually hitting a legitimate target, often by accident. Some in fact meritorious, including those for which he is harshly condemned across the spectrum; notably his willingness, pretty much, to accept the plea of the two Koreas in their historic declaration of April 2018 to move towards accommodation and disarmament "on their own accord," without external disruption, one of the few hopeful developments in world politics.

CHARLIE: I just want to go back to Trump and the issue of authoritarianism. You used strong language around the neo fascist stuff going on around the world now. What do you take away from the struggle in Germany after the end of Weimar and so forth? Trump may end up simply crushing with brute repression a lot of the left forces. You say you don't think that's likely? You don't see Trump's authoritarianism as leading to a rise of police state? When you go to protest these days, very often you're in these gated areas which are way away from the thing. It's hard to protest anywhere near the elite meetings and government offices.

NOAM: You weren't in the south in the '60s. It was much worse then. Incomparably worse. Under Obama, you didn't have cases where when there was a demonstration, people are being beaten bloody by the state police. They try to get up to the steps of the federal building for protection and the federal marshals threw them back to be beaten by the police. We're not seeing that. It's quite different.

CHARLIE: You're imagining that under a Trump administration, even given the people he's appointed at the justice department, the outright and brutal rhetoric we're hearing, you're saying that the environment for relatively free expression, is going to sustain itself so that the left really is going to have an opportunity to continue to do…

NOAM: Again, there isn't much point predicting. I think there's certainly good chances for it. I think the achievements and civil rights are pretty deeply ingrained. I don't think we're going to have anything like what we've seen in the past. For example, there's no indication now that there's anything like Wilson's Red Scare. I don't think that likely to occur. It's very unlikely that there's be anything like the Kennedy, Johnson, Nixon repression. There's no indication of that. There really has been progress. If you can defend those rights, which we should, I don't see any reason to expect real neo fascism. Could happen, but I don't think the indications are strong.

We shouldn't be frightened of it. We should proceed with the opportunities we have which are considerable. Others can be brought in as well. The repressive forces themselves can be undermined. That's happened often. They have shared interest in many ways. If demonstrations and other activities are taken with an eye toward reaching out to those who are unsympathetic and bringing them in, I think a lot of progress can be made. That's often happened. That aspect of it doesn't really seem to be an imminent danger. Could happen but doesn't seem to me as something that should be impeding us in anything we do.

9 Activists, Movements, and Electoral Politics

The Critique of Anti-Trumpism

*Noam Chomsky, Charles Derber,
Suren Moodliar, and Paul Shannon*

CHARLIE: Has the Left begun to learn any lessons from Trump's victory in 2016? How might it reconnect with the white working class? Is it important to do so? Are electoral politics key? Do we need an "united front" of the Left and Democratic Party office-holders or candidates?

NOAM: The Democrats (who are not "the left" by any means) essentially abandoned the working class by the 1970s, and that continues to the present. Thus Democrats were greatly cheered by their perceived success in the 2018 mid-term elections, when they were able to flip affluent suburban voters who are disgusted by Trump's antics—while again abandoning working people to their bitter class enemy. There have been moments when white working class voters thought that the Democrats might represent their interests. Many voted for Obama in 2008, believing his message of "hope" and "change," but were quickly disillusioned, realizing that they had once again been abandoned. In the regressive US political system, it is not easy for a third party to participate in electoral politics, but there are ways through fusion candidates and the like, and it may be possible for left activists to shift the Democratic Party in more social democratic directions, responding authentically to the very real and pressing needs of the majority of the population who have been victims of the neoliberal policies of the past generation. Those policies have sharply concentrated wealth while real wages have stagnated or worse. And benefits have declined along with the "growing worker insecurity" hailed by Fed chair Alan Greenspan when he was explaining to Congress the achievements of the great economy he was administering in the Clinton years. The remarkable success of the 2016 Sanders campaign, breaking with over a century of history of mostly bought elections, is an indication of what can be done, and is in part being done with the election of young progressive candidates.

But for the left, the electoral system, while of significance, is a side concern. Its real continuing task is to foster the development of popular grass-roots movements, and crucially, to help revitalize the labor movement, bringing in the alienated and disillusioned workers who have been abandoned during the years of neoliberal globalization and harsh attacks on labor, from the bitterly anti-labor Reagan administration and on to the present escalating class war targeting workers' rights—even the right to receive one's paycheck. Expediting the enormous crimes of wage theft is one of the priorities of the major corporate lobby ALEC (American Legislative Exchange Council), devoted to stealth subversion of democracy and elementary human rights. These powerful assaults on elementary rights, ranging very widely through the domains of basic human concerns (education, health, employment, and more) have to be exposed and countered by militant popular action, perhaps linked to electoral politics but not subordinated to the political process.

CHARLES: Has the Left simply been absorbed by the "progressive wing" of the Democratic Party?

NOAM: To some extent perhaps, but we shouldn't underestimate the many effective actions undertaken by grass-roots organizations all over the country, the real hope for the future I think.

CHARLES: Why do you think young people are so attracted to your work—amazing how many flock to read and hear you. You often don't talk extensively about activism but your message catalyzes many activists. Have you figured out what is it about your work that attracts the young and also moves them to a passion to change the world?

Dewey Square, Boston, October 22, 2011. Chomsky teaching
a class at Occupy Boston's Free School University.
Photo by Matthew J. Lee/The Boston Globe via Getty Images

NOAM: Whether it's true or not, I can't say. But I
hope it is, to some extent at least. That passion is
certainly needed, desperately. Whatever contrib-
utes to it should be encouraged and amplified.

CHARLES: You've often said over the last decade
that activism remains as strong as in the sixties in
the US? Do you still believe that? If so, why does
the peace movement seem almost invisible and the
Left so marginalized? What do activists have to do
to gain more visibility, reshape the national conversation and achieve their aims of justice, peace
and prevention of extinction?

NOAM: Is that accurate? I'm not so sure. Congress has just recently—I think for the first time—exercised its powers to "direct the removal of the United States Armed forces from hostilities…that have not been authorized by Congress," namely in expediting the Saudi-UAE assault that is creating the horrendous humanitarian catastrophe in Yemen. Far too late, but an important step, which reflects the popular force of the peace movement and the left. The same forces lie behind the election of a number of progressive young mostly female candidates, and in general the pressure on the Democratic Party to shift from its donor-oriented policies towards a more social democratic stance directed to the general public interest. That seems to be "reshaping the national conversation" in valuable if still much too limited ways, and opening doors to more ambitious achievements.

CHARLIE: You mean using the electoral progressive office-holders to build the popular movements?

NOAM: Sanders and Warren have opened possibilities.

CHARLIE: To reach the public?

NOAM: And to carry out your activities, to carry out the activist work.

CHARLIE: Yes.

NOAM: When Sanders, let's say, makes a pro-union or pro-environment comment, you say, "Fine, let's pursue that in open spaces," probably well beyond what he intends. That's fine. Make use of the opportunities that are available and increase those opportunities. Working within the Democratic Party, let's say, to get progressive people in Congress opens spaces, which you can then use to enhance the space and to work forward on the issues that concern you. It doesn't mean taking this leader and saying, "Okay, I worship him or her," but rather, using the opportunities that they present to move forward.

CHARLIE: Let's take climate. Does moving forward mean getting a carbon tax passed through Congress, or does it mean awakening the general public to the connection between capitalism and climate and doing mass actions which would lead towards some sort of more transformative situation? Or is it both?

NOAM: The word that we should avoid, I think, is "or". These are complementary activities. If parts of the conservative corporate world say, "Look, we ought to have a carbon tax," I don't think we should say, "Okay, I'm opposed to it because you're in favor."

CHARLIE: Right.

NOAM: If you want to push that, fine, but that's just the beginning. That brings up awareness, which allows us to move maybe at the local level, at any level, to try to press forward to ensure that these gains will be maintained. Now, this is true on every issue. I mean, things that are being ignored right now are very dangerous.

CHARLIE: Many fear that the Democratic Party, the liberals on Cable tv, such as MSNBC, and even much of the Left is playing into Trump's hands by focusing on his personality antics and tweets rather than the underlying structural crises of the economy, US hegemony and the climate crisis. One might say that Trump is "playing" the Democrats and liberals by calling attention to his own outrageousness.

NOAM: Well, we have to distinguish the Democratic Party, which I wouldn't exactly say it's being played. It's playing along. It's playing along by diverting attention from the things that are really happening. There's a whole raft of them. I've already mentioned two or three, including legislation that's being pushed through to undermine workers' rights, to undermine the limited constraints on financial institutions, to destroy the Consumer Protection Agency step by step, putting aside the attack on the environment, which is wild, but not the main thing. The Democratic Party is focusing on, actually, the one thing in Trump's whole agenda which is more or less defensible. They're trying to reduce tensions with Russia. That's what they want to focus on. Is it being played or playing along? You can make your own decision.

CHARLIE: Would you generalize that from the Democratic Party... Now, I'm talking about anti-Trump activity. The Left grass movements in general, do you think they're also being sucked into a kind of focus on Trump?

NOAM: It's a mixture. Many are pursuing the goals that they should be doing seriously. In fact, I think probably the large majority, but a lot of what's visible is Trump, get rid of Trump, which is not the issue.

CHARLIE: What about the protest against Trump's travel ban or against the Women's March when he was elected? Do those fall into that same rubric of diversionary focus on Trump or not?

NOAM: Focus on the travel ban, yes, but why does Trump pick up a travel ban? He doesn't care one way or another who's in the country. He focuses on it because the base that he's constructed, he knows that that will win points with them.

CHARLIE: Absolutely.

NOAM: He's compelled to focus his attention on maintaining the loyalty, and by now, actually, the worship of the base. It's amazing to see. That's the cover under which all these other things can go on. So it makes sense to focus on the travel ban, but to look at where the roots of it are, where's it coming from?

CHARLIE: Which takes you beyond Trump to the larger systemic conditions.

NOAM: Why do states in the United States pass legislation banning Sharia law, which is about as likely to be implemented as I don't know what. Maybe the country being consumed by a lightning storm or something. These are all over the country. These are serious things, deeply rooted in large parts of the population that have to be addressed.

CHARLIE: Sure they do. Just one final thing on this. What about the people who say Trump is a threat? Who I think who would agree with you, but who would say his autocratic and kind of bonkers psychology that could lead to mass escalation in Korea or Iran or whatever. What would you say to them when they say we need some focus on Trump, one, because he's dangerous in that particular respect and, two, because he might be an avenue through which, as you say, you could really look at the underlying systemic forces.

NOAM: Well, let's take Korea. The world is well aware, and the elites are well aware, that there is a possible way to reduce extremely dangerous tensions. That's to respond positively to the Chinese, Russian, North Korean proposal for a double freeze. A North Korean freeze on weapons systems, a US freeze on threatening military maneuvers right on North Korea's border, which are no joke for them. That would be a first step towards entering negotiations. Well, the government has flatly rejected it. The UN just again rejected it, but so did the liberal commentators. Read Roger Cohen in the *New York Times*. Says absolutely can't do this. So this is not just Trump. It's much broader. We have to ask why the insistence that we must hold a sledgehammer over the head of anyone we don't like and keep threatening to destroy them and not pursue the diplomatic options that are available?

Can we consider what the record is of the United States and North Korea? I mean, it's devastating. North Korea was flattened by the United States back in the early 1950s. Destroyed. In fact, it was done with a real glee. You really have to read the *Air Force Quarterly Journal* or the official histories to see the joy with which they were describing, at the time, this magnificent site of huge dams being destroyed by American bombers—of course, a major war crime—water flooding the valleys and destroying the rice on which Asians, not just Koreans, depend for survival and so on. Maybe North Koreans don't read this stuff anymore, but they're aware of the sentiment and what it means: with nuclear-capable bombers flying right near their territory, it's not a joke. Maybe it's the worse country in the world. It certainly is high on the list of qualifying, but there are things that could be done. I mean, it is recognized, you can read it in the *Financial Times*, not Left-wing rags, the North

Koreans are seeking to develop their economy and have, in fact, had apparently—the statistics are almost meaningless—but it looks like a reasonable growth rate and moves toward economic development. The military burden is a huge impediment to that. That offers possibilities for serious negotiation, which are much more serious than getting into a trade war with China, which will devastate this country and everyone else. The point is there are options that could be pursued. They're barely being discussed. When they are, they're mostly rejected, and it's not just Trump. It's much broader.

CHARLIE: What validates your view, generally, is that the people who are engaged in purely fighting Trump, they call him a child and the people that carried out this devastating history—Mattis and McMaster, all the generals—are viewed as the, quote, "adults in the room." Suddenly, they end up, in the name of opposing Trump, legitimating the entire structural history, the history you've been describing.

NOAM: We have a great way of suppressing the history that we don't like. This is live. It's not ancient history. It's not something that happened in the 15th century.

CHARLIE: One last question. Is there anything positive you'd want to say about the anti-Trump resistance?

NOAM: In so far as the anti-Trump resistance is focusing on the issues, on the roots in the population,
including much of the liberal population, so far as
doing that, that makes sense. When it personalizes
it and says look how stupid and crazy this guy is...
that's playing into his hands, because that's what
he wants. That's his role. His role is to take attention away from what's going on.

10 Activism in the Age of Extinction

Noam Chomsky, Charles Derber,
Suren Moodliar, and Paul Shannon

CHARLIE: Extinction and the contemplation thereof has a paralyzing and demobilizing potential. How then should we talk about power and activism in the age of extinction?

NOAM: Realistically. The threats are very serious, and reactions cannot be delayed. It's worth noting that the Trump administration is fully aware of the impending disaster. In what may qualify as the most evil document in history, naturally from a bureaucracy, a recent Trump environmental impact study estimated that by the end of the century temperatures will have increased by 7 degrees (F), with accompanying sea level rise and other disasters of almost unimaginable proportions. The study therefore calls for eliminating fuel efficiency standards for cars and light trucks, so as to accelerate the disaster. The reasoning is straightforward: what's the difference, since we're going off the cliff anyway. The tacit assumption is that the rest of the world is also criminally insane and will join us in fiddling while the planet burns, putting poor

Nero in the shadows. Trump himself is a firm believer in global warming. He revealed that when he petitioned the government of Ireland to build a wall to protect his golf course from rising sea levels caused by global warming.

We can say the same about the titans of finance and industry. The CEO of JPMorgan Chase, Jamie Dimon, is an intelligent and literate person, who is surely aware of the facts—as he sharply increases investment in fossil fuels. This attitude generalizes throughout the economic system, which is designed for suicide.

But the fact that the leadership is happy to consign us to catastrophe for the benefit of short-term profit doesn't entail that we must go along politely. Rather, a realistic assessment of the threats and of the announced policies should be accompanied by concrete proposals, in part already being implemented, to contain the threats and to create a much better and more livable society. It's not hard, for example, to think of more pleasant ways to spend one's time than in many hours of traffic jams commuting to work on Boston's Southeast Expressway. And much more. A much better life is within reach by measures to mitigate the serious threats to survival: Robert Pollin's proposals for a green economy, to mention an informed and promising analysis. Furthermore, bearing in mind Bakunin's advice to construct the germs of a better future society within the present deeply flawed one, we can at the same time be engaged in efforts to gain for ourselves and to try to extend to others understanding of why and how radical social change should be carried out. And we can proceed beyond to develop elements of it: worker-owned enterprises, cooperatives, localism in agricultural production, and much else.

11 The Movement and Third Parties

Noam Chomsky, Charles Derber,
Suren Moodliar, and Paul Shannon

CHARLIE: When you talk about this organized left community... do you have a more concrete image of what that looks like? Is that labor unions that are oriented toward work? There have been co-ops that have unions in them of course. Does it mean environmental movements and antiracist movements becoming part of a unified...

NOAM: All of that but even more than that. It can also be a serious independent party. In the US system, which happens to be very regressive by comparative standards, it's very hard for an independent party to enter the political system, but it's not impossible. If an authentic independent political party would develop, it could become an electoral alternative. That means a party that doesn't just show up every four years and say, I have a candidate for the election. It means starting at the local levels. School boards, town meetings, state legislatures, house representatives, all the way. In some of these House of Representatives districts, a very small amount of money is enough to win the election. Many of them run unopposed. State legislature is the same situation.

CHARLIE: Ralph Nader has been making this argument, that through district by district organizing, a small number of people could elect a progressive. There's a lot of debate about whether this is creating an independent party or working with some of the Sanders people to align with progressive Democrats. What's your view of how to think about that?

NOAM: I don't think you have to make a decision on that. You can try both and see which one succeeds. They're not different.

CHARLIE: You think it's worth moving in both directions?

NOAM: I think it's worth trying everything you can. If the Democratic Party could be taken away from the party bosses, the huge funders, the Democratic machine, and turned into a popular party, fine. If an independent party...

CHARLIE: In your personal view, is that a realistic possibility? Could Sanders, Warren, some of these new people trying to get the democratic establishment out and dig into the labor movement, is this worth doing in your view? Given that the culture of the country and the whole...

NOAM: It's worth doing and it's not an alternative to trying to develop an independent party. Both should be done. They could even cooperate.

CHARLIE: It's interesting because when I hear this conversation very often on the left, it breaks down, very often, into a choice. People feel you're going to go for the Green Party, you're going to build up independent parties or you're going to try to work for Democrats... and there are people who feel this is a choice that has to be made.

NOAM: An individual has to make a choice. A person can't do everything. The movements can do both. They can even be integrated, mutually supportive. Push the Democratic Party as far as possible toward a progressive direction. When it gets to a point that's not far enough, there's something independent which can in fact influence them. If an independent, a third party develops, it's kind of how the labor party long ago developed in England or the NDP in Canada. It can have an influence on what the major parties do and even become a major party. These possibilities are not inconceivable.

This is only one stream. This should be going on alongside of many other activist efforts: for example, the effort say to get to worker ownership in Taunton or at a large-scale level to shift the whole auto industry toward what it ought to be, which could have been done had there been some kind of activist left we're talking about. I think there's a basis for developing those kinds of efforts.

CHARLIE: I think you're saying there's a very pluralistic set of possibilities for the communities we're talking about. You're saying you're weary of pinning the hopes on one thing, like the Democratic Party or a Green Party... You want to see a mushrooming of everything you can to build these alternatives.

NOAM: A healthy left would be one in which individuals of course follow what they're good at, what makes sense to them, what fits into their life and so on. You have to make choices. You can't do everything. It should be that each of those individuals should recognize that the many other choices are parallel and mutually supportive and we can get together...

12 Overcoming Isolation and Powerlessness

Movements and Community

Noam Chomsky, Charles Derber,
Suren Moodliar, and Paul Shannon

CHARLIE: For my final question, and we've talked before about this, you noted that a lot of the institutions like the union movement and so forth, which brought people who were atomized and isolated together in various settings have been deliberately weakened by right-wing forces—unions in particular. I guess the question is: when you talk about people personally engaging these overwhelming issues, many people feel very atomized and isolated. We need to get them together.

NOAM: That's right.

CHARLIE: Young people. There was just a study that said the biggest problem on campuses these days, they're among students, but 30% of all college students are feeling alone, lonely, isolated.

NOAM: They're alone on their iPads.

CHARLIE: On their iPads?

NOAM: Yup.

CHARLIE: Isolated people find it hard to engage, because they feel "I just don't have the power to..." Do you see any sort of solution?

NOAM: Sure, see it all the time.

We happen to be geared to electoral politics by massive propaganda, but in fact, look what happened. At the time of the Sanders campaign, it got enormous support from young people. In fact, right now (in 2016), Sanders is the most popular political figure in the country by a huge margin, mostly among young people. That energized people for a political campaign. Some of it is going on into groups growing out of the campaign that are doing quite constructive work. The environmental movement is organizing great numbers of people. DACA is going to, I'm sure, have enormous popular support. If there's something that people feel I can do something about, then they become involved. And there are many such things. The role of Left activists is to bring to people the understanding that, yes, you can do something. There are many ways of doing this. Focusing on something very local like something that's going wrong in my college cafeteria. Let's work on that. If you can achieve that, you can say, "Okay, we can do something. Let's go on to the next thing."

Part 3

100 Seconds to Midnight

The pandemic, for all its horrors, has a silver lining. It has brought to popular consciousness some of the roots of a wide range of social maladies, and exposed them to challenge. It has revealed the human qualities that can open the way to a much better world. The courage and dedication of health workers, often with barely minimal facilities and protection, is truly inspiring. The same is true of the ways that communities have been organizing to help those in need and to fill the spaces left by failing institutions. The shift in values from personal gain to mutual aid could be a basis for broad changes of consciousness with far-reaching import.

In the United States, activist movements have provided dramatic examples of what can be achieved. To take just *one* case, a *Green* New Deal, in some form, is essential for survival. A few *years* ago, it was hardly more than an object of mainstream ridicule. Today it is on the legislative agenda...

It is the right time to keep firmly in mind the slogan that Gramsci made famous: Pessimism of the intellect, Optimism of the will. And to act on it, forcefully and decisively. Anything less will be a fateful error.

13 Confronting Climate Change, War, and Pandemics in the Trump Era

Noam Chomsky

It was not in doubt that 2020 would be a fateful year, especially so for those who care enough about the world to try to determine its fate—for activists, in brief.

One reason is that 2020 brings us an election in the most powerful state in world history. Its outcome will have a major impact not only on the United States, but thanks to US power, on the perils faced by the entire world.

The nature and scale of these perils was underscored at the year's outset when the hands of the famous Doomsday Clock were set, providing as good a succinct assessment as we have of the state of the world. Since Donald Trump's election, the minute hand has been moved steadily toward midnight, meaning "it's over." As 2020 opened, the analysts abandoned minutes and turned to seconds: 100 seconds to midnight, the closest to terminal disaster since the first setting of the Clock in the wake of the atom bomb attacks. The reasons were the usual ones: the severe and increasing threat of nuclear war and of environmental catastrophe (with the White House proudly in the lead in racing to the abyss) and the deterioration of functioning democracy, the one hope for dealing with impending disaster.

There is time to save organized human society (and many other species) from cataclysm, but not much. How much depends in no small measure on the US election in November 2020, which may turn out to be the most important election in human history, perhaps coming close to sealing the fate of organized human society.

Extreme words, but are they an exaggeration? Four more years of Trumpism might raise global warming to irreversible tipping points. At the very least it would sharply raise the costs of achieving some measure of decent survival. Trump's dismantling of the thin barriers to nuclear destruction might well succeed in setting off a final war; and even if not, will drive the world closer to the brink. Another term will also provide Mitch McConnell with more time to pursue his assault on democracy by cramming the judiciary with enough young far-right justices to ensure that deeply reactionary and destructive policies will persist no matter what the public would prefer. All three of the dire threats that led to the move of the minute hand toward midnight are targets of Trump and the party that is now in his pocket, dedicated to intensifying them.

Left to Right: Charles Derber, Randall Wallace, Noam Chomsky, and Valeria Chomsky. Old South Church, Boston, April 11, 2019. Noam returns to Boston to issue a call to action around climate, nuclear war and the crisis of democracy.
Photo by Pat Westwater-Jong.

For these reasons alone—there are many others—every effort must be expended to prevent this tragedy; and if it occurs, to redouble efforts to limit the damage and open the way to a livable world.

The Doomsday Clock analysts could have added a fourth reason for advancing the hand toward midnight: the tepid response to the growing threat to "the survival of humanity"—the words of a memo of JPMorgan Chase, America's largest bank, warning of

what lies ahead on our current course.[1] Trump's escalation of the threat of terminal nuclear war barely
received a whisper during the political campaign of
2019–2020. There has been some mention of Trump's
enthusiastic race toward environmental catastrophe,
but it is not ranked high among his crimes though it
vastly exceeds those that arouse great rancor. Republicans meanwhile continue on their merry course of
playing down the threat as they have been doing for a
decade, ever since bribes and intimidation by the Koch
brothers juggernaut abruptly ended their small steps
toward caring about the fate of the country and human
society generally. The impact on the public is clear in
polls: barely a quarter of Republicans regard this imminent threat to the survival of humanity as an urgent
problem, or even agree that humans have some role in
"climate change" (the preferred euphemism for global
warming in public discourse, interpretable as a flood in
my back yard rather than the survival of humanity).[2]

1 Greenfield, Patrick, and Jonathan Watts. "JP Morgan Economists Warn Climate Crisis Is Threat to Human Race." *The
   Guardian*, February 21, 2020, sec. Environment. https://
   www.theguardian.com/environment/2020/feb/21/jp-
   morgan-economists-warn-climate-crisis-threat-human-
   race.
2 Kennedy, Brian. "U.S. Concern about Climate Change
   Is Rising, but Mainly among Democrats." Pew Research
   Center (blog). Accessed February 13, 2020. https://www.
   pewresearch.org/fact-tank/2020/04/16/u-s-concern-about-
   climate-change-is-rising-but-mainly-among-democrats/.

Trump himself, glorying in personal power, seems to be enjoying the spectacle. He quite openly thumbs his nose at the victims he is working to destroy—surely with eyes open, and with hands outstretched to the coffers of his primary constituency of private wealth and corporate power. One sordid illustration is a White House announcement that the President is becoming interested in climate change and is reading a book to become better informed. They even released the title: "Donald J. Trump: An Environmental Hero."[3]

It is hard to doubt that that is a gesture of contempt by the self-declared "chosen one" (eyes raised to heaven before an adoring crowd, which ranks him the greatest president in history, their savior).

I'm old enough to remember the radio broadcasts of Hitler's Nuremberg rallies, not understanding the words though the mood and import were unmistakable. Trump's rallies cannot fail to revive these childhood memories. We should, however, be wary of the temptation to invoke fascism. Nazism had an ideology, a horrific one, including mass slaughter of Jews and other undesirables and military conquest, but also Party control of all aspects of life, the business world included. That's almost the opposite of the neoliberal

3 Friedman, Lisa. "A Trillion Trees: How One Idea Triumphed Over Trump's Climate Denialism." *The New York Times*, February 12, 2020, sec. Climate. https://www.nytimes.com/2020/02/12/climate/trump-trees-climate-change.html.

reality of which Trump is the current champion. Donald J. has a much simpler ideology: ME!!!

Trump's antics are tolerated by those whom Adam Smith called "the masters of mankind"—in his day, the merchants and manufacturers of England, in ours, multinational corporations and financial institutions, called "the masters of the universe" in our more expansive times. The masters tolerate the freak show in the White House as long as the chief manipulator is at least disciplined enough to pour dollars into their overstuffed pockets, the main thrust of his "populist" policies.

Reinvigorating the arms race also seems to be a gratifying experience for the chosen one, unsullied by its likely outcome. It surely is a welcome gift to military industry, which is openly exulting about the lavish taxpayer gifts for creating even more awesome means to destroy us all; and also, a little down the road, further gifts to devise some (hopeless) means of defending against the new means of destruction that enemies are invited to develop. Even a return to the days of Eisenhower and Reagan would offer at least some respite, perhaps time to bring this horror to an end.

These are no trifling matters. The survival of humanity depends in no small measure on how they are resolved.

The year 2020 opened with further warnings. Health specialist Helen Epstein wrote that "The United States is in the throes of a colossal health crisis," citing a death toll of "roughly 190,000 lives each year." The leading British medical journal, *The Lancet* estimated 68,000 extra deaths in the United States. To this we may add the considerably greater toll of unnecessary deaths in the collapsing private nursing homes that are another of Trump's delights, run by executives who are a great source of funding for his re-election campaign as he sharply reduces regulations that require them to provide some minimal care.[4]

Epstein and the *Lancet* scientists were writing just before the outbreak of the Covid-19 pandemic. The deregulation of the nursing homes was also in the works earlier, but proceeded as patients were dying from the coronavirus pandemic. Epstein was referring to the unique American malady termed "deaths of despair," studied in depth by economists Anne Case

---

4   Epstein, Helen. "Left Behind." *The New York Review*, March 26, 2020. https://www.nybooks.com/articles/2020/03/26/left-behind-life-expectancy-crisis/.

Galvani, Alison P., Alyssa S. Parpia, Eric M. Foster, Burton H. Singer, and Meagan C. Fitzpatrick. "Improving the Prognosis of Health Care in the USA." *The Lancet 395*, no. 10223 (February 15, 2020): 524–33. https://doi.org/10.1016/S0140-6736(19)33019-3.

Drucker, Jesse, and Jessica Silver-Greenberg. "Trump Administration Is Relaxing Oversight of Nursing Homes." *The New York Times*, March 14, 2020, sec. Business. https://www.nytimes.com/2020/03/14/business/trump-administration-nursing-homes.html.

and Angus Deaton, "concentrated in the rusted-out factory towns and depressed rural areas left behind by globalization, automation, and downsizing." The *Lancet* study was concerned with another tragedy unique to the United States among developed societies: deaths from lack of adequate insurance (or any at all). This is happening in the richest society of the world, with incomparable advantages, but suffering under a private-for-profit health system with twice the per capita expenses of comparable societies and some of the worst health outcomes.

The health system has been a prime target for Trump-McConnell and their party, committed to making the tragedy even more bitter by ridding the country of Obama's Affordable Care Act and returning to the considerably worse situation before (rhetoric aside). They were not able to achieve that, but they did manage to modify the ACA by offering low cost high co-pay plans with limited coverage, making it impossible for many to afford the cost of test and treatment in our dysfunctional healthcare system, thus enhancing the spread of the pandemic. We return to other Trump contributions to this end.

The limited attention to the existential perils faded even further, to virtual invisibility, as the new health crisis struck, almost completely dominating commentary. Understandably. It is severe indeed. It has virtually closed down global society, causing immense harm. In the United States, it struck a society that was already "in the throes of a colossal health crisis," not a natural crisis but a socioeconomic and political one, a crisis with considerably broader scope.

These are matters that have to be carefully explored and understood if further catastrophes are to be avoided. As the crisis fades, the question of how to reconstruct the battered societies will gain increasing prominence. For activists, the task was articulated succinctly by author and journalist Vijay Prashad, the regular voice of the miserable of the earth: "We won't go back to normal, because normal is the problem."[5]

To accomplish this necessary task, we have to proceed from a clear understanding of the Trump malignancy, but far more: the rot from which it grew, the institutional structure on which it rests, and the cultural-ideological climate that sustains it.

While attending to these critical matters, we cannot overlook the vast difference between the coronavirus horrors and the existential crises that inform the setting of the Doomsday Clock.

There have been severe health crises in human history. The Swine Flu (H1N1) pandemic, first identified in the United States in 2009, killed from 150,000 to almost 600,000 people in the first year alone according to the Center for Disease Control, 80% of them under 65. The first H1N1 pandemic ("the Spanish

5 Prashad, Vijay. "We Won't Go Back to Normal, Because Normal Was the Problem: The Thirteenth Newsletter." The Tricontinental (blog), March 28, 2020. https://www.thetricontinental.org/newsletterissue/newsletter-13-2020-new-world-order/.

Flu") a century ago is estimated to have killed 30–100 million people. The 14th century Black Death brought horrifying death to a third or more of Europeans, sowing panic and despair.

Europe recovered. And soon attained a higher level. The labor shortage led to technological advances. Soon Europe was powerful enough to become the scourge of the earth, undertaking the worst genocidal crimes of history as European savagery and filth devastated the Western hemisphere, destroying tens of millions of people and advanced civilizations. There was no recovery under colonization and extermination.

Spared the bitter fate of imperial domination, Europe itself did recover. The world will recover from the current pandemic, possibly at horrendous human cost. There will be no recovery from the advance of global warming or from major nuclear war, though they do not disrupt daily life too much, at least for the more privileged, until it is too late.

At its root the Covid-19 pandemic results from a colossal market failure, much like the vastly more serious environmental crisis. It had been known for years that a pandemic was likely. The SARS epidemic of 2003 was caused by a similar coronavirus. Its genome was soon sequenced and vaccines were developed though they did not proceed beyond the pre-clinical level. That should have helped to investigate related viruses like today's culprit and to develop defenses and cures, at least to have prepared facilities for dealing with a major crisis. Big Pharma had little interest. Following good capitalist logic, it adhered to market signals, which dictate that there is no profit in preparing for a catastrophic crisis. Health institutions kept to business–style concepts of efficiency: no fat in the system, so any disruption causes catastrophe.

The pathology of capitalist logic is revealed by the lack of ventilators, one of the major killers as the pandemic spread. The Obama administration had contracted with a firm that was producing inexpensive high quality ventilators. It was bought by a large corporation, Covidien, which sidelined the project, perhaps to block competition with its own expensive ventilators, not an unusual corporate practice.[6] Soon after,

> In 2014, with no ventilators having been delivered to the government, Covidien executives told officials at the [Federal] biomedical research agency that they wanted to get out of the contract, according to three former federal officials. The executives complained that it was not sufficiently profitable for the company.[7]

6 Cunningham, Colleen and Ederer, Florian and Ma, Song, Killer Acquisitions (April 19, 2020). *Journal of Political Economy*, forthcoming, Available at SSRN: https://ssrn.com/abstract=3241707 or http://dx.doi.org/10.2139/ssrn.3241707
7 Kulish, Nicholas, Sarah Kliff, and Jessica Silver-Greenberg. "The U.S. Tried to Build a New Fleet of Ventilators. The Mission Failed." *The New York Times*, March 29, 2020, sec. Business. https://www.nytimes.com/2020/03/29/business/coronavirus-us-ventilator-shortage.html.

In a functioning society, the government could have taken over to overcome the gross market failure, which caused havoc when the pandemic struck. But that is impermissible under neoliberal principles. As *The New York Times* commented, with suitable understatement,

> The stalled efforts to create a new class of cheap, easy-to-use ventilators highlight the perils of outsourcing projects with critical public-health implications to private companies; their focus on maximizing profits is not always consistent with the government's goal of preparing for a future crisis.

Or more accurately, it is a recipe for disaster, dismissing the ritual bow to the government's necessarily benign goals.

It's worth noting that the looming environmental crisis is also accelerated by market signals. Chevron closed profitable renewable energy projects because the killings from oil and gas were greater still. ExxonMobil didn't follow suit. It had never even devoted funds to such marginalia as preserving life on earth. We learn from the business press that

> In a March [2014] report on carbon risk to shareholders, ExxonMobil (XOM) argued that its laser-like focus on fossil fuels is a sound strategy, regardless of climate change, because the world

needs vastly more energy and the likelihood of significant carbon reductions is 'highly unlikely'.[8]

Investors are led in the same direction. Decarbonization is essential for decent survival. There are companies developing methods, but they are starved of funds. Any returns would be far off. For enterprising venture capitalists, there's much more profit in adding new bells and whistles to I-phones.

The fault is not with individuals. These are the rules of the game for those parts of the economy that observe market principles.

Returning to the pandemic, the government could have filled the gap as it has often done, including the huge taxpayer-funded development of the basis for today's high tech economy and the regular bailouts of the culprits in the crashes that have been a hallmark of the neoliberal era. The familiar story is being replicated today as corporate leaders come hat in hand to the nanny state after having made use of the good times to enrich themselves with stock buybacks, skyrocketing executive pay, and the other devices that over 40 years have created a society in which more than 20% of wealth is in the hands of 0.1% of the population while most workers live from paycheck to paycheck and half the population has negative net worth.

8 Elgin, Ben. "Chevron Dims the Lights on Renewable Energy Projects." BusinessWeek, May 29, 2020. https://www.bloomberg.com/news/articles/2014-05-29/chevron-dims-the-lights-on-renewable-energy-projects.

"We know the United States does not have Medicare for all," Thomas Ferguson and Rob Johnson comment on the latest episode, but "there is no reason why it should have one sided single payer insurance for corporations." Not a necessity, as they explain, outlining simple ways to overcome this form of corporate robbery of the public. But these are doctrinally excluded.[9]

9 Friedman, Zack. "78% Of Workers Live Paycheck To Paycheck." Forbes, January 11, 2019. https://www.forbes.com/sites/zackfriedman/2019/01/11/live-paycheck-to-paycheck-government-shutdown/.

Steverman, Ben. "The Wealth Detective Who Finds the Hidden Money of the Super Rich." Bloomberg.Com, May 23, 2019. https://www.bloomberg.com/news/features/2019-05-23/the-wealth-detective-who-finds-the-hidden-money-of-the-super-rich.

Saez, Emmanuel, and Gabriel Zucman. The Triumph of Injustice: How the Rich Dodge Taxes and How to Make Them Pay. First Edition. New York, NY: W. W. Norton & Company, 2019.

Ferguson, Thomas, and Rob Johnson. "Rule Number 1 for Government Bailouts of Companies: Make Sure Voters and Taxpayers Share in the Upside." Institute for New Economic Thinking. Accessed November 13, 2020. https://www.ineteconomics.org/perspectives/blog/rule-number-1-for-government-bailouts-of-companies-make-sure-voters-and-taxpayers-share-in-the-upside.

As an aside, contrary to general belief the United States does enjoy universal health care. It is called "emergency rooms," required by law to treat everyone who can make it there, the most cruel, expensive, and inefficient form of "medicare for all." And a benefit that will soon have much wider reach, it seems, as millions are expected to lose health insurance with job loss. Another "American peculiarity," Emmanuel Saez and Gabriel Zucman point out, traceable to the unusually weak social welfare systems in the United States:

> throughout the world, governments are protecting employment. Workers keep their jobs, even in industries that are shut down. The government covers most of their wage through direct payments to employers. Wages are, in effect, socialized for the duration of the crisis.

Again, doctrinally unacceptable in what has long been a business-run society to an unusual extent, thereby striking further blows in the neoliberal era, with bipartisan support.[10]

Also doctrinally excluded, as noted, was the sensible step of government initiatives to fill the gap

10 LaVito. "Lose Your Job, Lose Your Insurance: Coronavirus Hits Health Plans - Bloomberg." Bloomberg.Com, March 26, 2020. https://www.bloomberg.com/news/articles/2020-03-26/mass-job-losses-threaten-to-leave-millions-in-u-s-uninsured.

opened by drastic market failure. That too was barred by the plague that afflicted the United States and Britain, then the world, about 40 years ago: the neoliberal version of savage capitalism. Reagan informed us with his sunny smile that "government is the problem"—meaning that decisions have to be removed from an institution that is under some public influence and transferred to the unaccountable private tyrannies that were handing Reagan his script. Milton Friedman and other luminaries explained that the public good is not the concern of private power: rather pure greed. Meanwhile Margaret Thatcher assured us that "there is no society," only individuals facing the rigors of the market on their own. As Anatole France elucidated the "libertarian" principle in a famous adage, the rich man and the poor man must be equally free to sleep under the bridge at night. And furthermore, Thatcher sternly added, "there is no alternative" to this state of affairs, which has brought ruin to much of the world in ways there should be no need to review here.

Unwittingly no doubt, Thatcher was paraphrasing Karl Marx, who condemned the autocratic rulers of his day for trying to turn the population to a "sack of potatoes," atomized individuals lacking ways to

Saez, Emmanuel, and Gabriel Zucman. "Opinion | Jobs Aren't Being Destroyed This Fast Elsewhere. Why Is That?" *The New York Times*, March 30, 2020, sec. Opinion. https://www.nytimes.com/2020/03/30/opinion/coronavirus-economy-saez-zucman.html.

interact with others to form ideas and programs and to act together to interfere with the preferred doctrine of government of, for, and by wealth and corporate power.

One consequence in England has been the systematic conversion of what had long been ranked as the world's best health system, the National Health Service, to something like the worst health system of the developed world, the profit-governed privatized US healthcare system. Apart from its numerous other failings, this system is singularly unprepared to deal with a crisis. Just-on-time methods may be fine for manufacturing. For health care, they are a disaster in the waiting: and as I personally and I'm sure many others can attest from personal experience, not just in the waiting. Hospital beds, nurses, ventilators, staffs, other facilities must be limited to what is normally expected. Any fat in the system would not be cost-effective, the supreme ideal.

The consequences become dramatically evident as soon as something goes wrong. We saw that at once as the pandemic erupted, exacerbated by the outlandish reaction from the White House. One consequence is that because of the radical inadequacy of testing, US authorities had little idea even how far the disease had spread. The *South China Morning Post* (Hong Kong) provides an authoritative daily report on the global spread of infection. In their charts, one country is listed with an asterisk signifying "includes presumptive cases." For all others, the WHO has the data. In the citadel of neoliberalism, the government can't even collect the data, let alone provide the needed facilities or a coordinated response.

It's important to bear in mind that neoliberalism is a flexible doctrine. Sometimes government most definitely is the answer in such ways as those already mentioned, and many others. Thus while it would be improper for the government to infringe upon the rights of Big Pharma by developing drugs and vaccines to protect people from pandemics, it is laudatory to provide drug companies with exorbitant patent rights in the mislabeled "free trade agreements" (TRIPS), guaranteeing huge profits and raising the costs of drugs far beyond what they should be under rational arrangements.[11]

Government is also the answer to enforce good behavior, with extreme violence if necessary, in the interests of "sound economics"—an interesting concept that I'll put aside. The gurus of neoliberalism—Ludwig von Mises, Friedrich Hayek, and others—welcomed the vicious Pinochet dictatorship with enthusiasm. Earlier, von Mises could scarcely contain his delight when unions and social democracy were destroyed in

---

11 On this matter see particularly Baker, Dean. Rigged: How Globalization and the Rules of the Modern Economy Were Structured to Make the Rich Richer. Washington, D.C.: Center for Economic and Policy Research, 2017. available at www.cepr.net.

the 1920s by the proto-fascist Austrian regime that he soon joined.

State violence is quite compatible with neoliberal principles, a lesson worth remembering as the world recovers and new paths are explored to construct a new society from the wreckage.

Administration concerns for the health and welfare of the population were spelled out in Trump's budget proposal, released on February 10 while the pandemic was raging. As reviewed by historian Lawrence Wittner,

> The budget calls for deep cuts in major U.S. government programs, especially those protecting public health. The Department of Health and Human Services would be slashed by 10 percent, while the Centers for Disease Control and Prevention, which has already been proven to be underfunded and unprepared to deal with the coronavirus outbreak, would be cut by a further 9 percent. Spending on Medicaid, which currently insures healthcare for one out of five Americans, would plummet by roughly $900 billion, largely thanks to reductions in coverage for the poor and the disabled. Meanwhile, Medicare expenditures would drop by roughly $500 billion. The budget proposal's reshuffling of agency responsibilities in connection with tobacco regulation also seems likely to contribute to a decline in public health.

Virtually every program that helps mere people, particularly the poor and vulnerable, gets the axe, while the bloated military and border control are to grow substantially. And to drive another nail in the coffin of viable existence, "the budget promotes a fossil fuel 'energy boom' in the United States, including an increase in the production of natural gas and crude oil."[12]

This is after 4 years of "deep cuts to science," the journal *Science* reports, "including cuts to funding for the Centers for Disease Control and Prevention and the NIH" among others; "all to support political goals—the nation has had nearly 4 years of harming and ignoring science," with particularly harmful effects for health and the environment needed to sustain life.[13] Meanwhile, as the United States reaches the highest death toll in the world, Trump's EPA races

---

12 Wittner, Lawrence. "Trump's Budget Proposal Reveals His Values | History News Network." History News Network, March 15, 2020. https://historynewsnetwork.org/article/174577.

   "What's in President Trump's Fiscal 2021 Budget?" *The New York Times*, February 10, 2020, sec. Business. https://www.nytimes.com/2020/02/10/business/economy/trump-budget-explained-facts.html.

13 Thorp, H. Holden. "Do Us a Favor." *Science* 367, no. 6483 (March 13, 2020): 1169–1169. https://doi.org/10.1126/science.abb6502.

to eliminate regulations that preserve life and health, much to the glee of the corporate sectors that now virtually run it.

The timing and character of the actions of the EPA reflect Trump's keen sense of how to harm the living and destroy the lives of future generations. As the pandemic raced out of control and even the self-confessed stable genius was compelled to withdraw his rosy predictions and call for lockdown,

> The Trump administration on Tuesday [March 31] took the final step in its three-year quest to dismantle Obama-era fuel-economy and greenhouse gas emissions regulations for automobiles, a process that has fractured carmakers, enraged environmentalists and sparked courtroom battles. Under a rule unveiled March 31, the administration will require automakers to boost the fuel efficiency of new cars by 1.5% per year through 2026, a major relaxation of previous mandates demanding improvements of roughly 5% annually.

Apart from the long-term impact on global warming, this latest effort to destroy the legacy of the hated Obama will contribute to the "over 30,000 deaths and reduced life expectancy" annually associated with air pollution in the United States."[14]

14 Beene, Ryan, Jennifer A. Dlouhy, and Keith Naughton. "Trump Chides 'Foolish' Car Executives After Easing Mileage Rules." Bloomberg.com, March 31, 2020. https://

Is the term "sociopath" too strong? And what is the right term for the loyal courtiers in "the world's greatest deliberative body"?

The budget was released after officials were well aware of what was happening; long after, in fact, if at least someone has survived in Trump's circles who follows current health news. On December 31, China informed the World Health Organization of cases of pneumonia of undetermined etiology. Within a week China informed the WHO that it was a coronavirus and that its scientists had sequenced the genome, and offered the information to others.[15] That's long before Trump assured the country that it was just flu, that it was all contained, that he gets a 10 out of 10 for his brilliant reaction, that it's out of control and he was the first one to know it was a pandemic, and the rest of the astonishing performance.

---

www.bloomberg.com/news/articles/2020-03-31/trump-wraps-up-three-year-effort-to-weaken-auto-efficiency-rules.

ScienceDaily. "Air Pollution in US Associated with over 30,000 Deaths and Reduced Life Expectancy." Accessed November 13, 2020. https://www.sciencedaily.com/releases/2019/07/190723142937.htm.

15 "Novel Coronavirus (2019-NCoV) Situation Report - 1." World Health Organization, January 21, 2020. https://www.who.int/docs/default-source/coronaviruse/situation-reports/20200121-sitrep-1-2019-ncov.pdf.

Minimal concern for the welfare of the general population would have led the administration to act quickly on the information provided by China. Pandemics had long been predicted by scientists. For years, US intelligence agencies had been warning about the increasing risks of a global pandemic. That continued up to the outbreak. "In a worldwide threats assessment in 2018 and 2017, intelligence analysts even mentioned a close cousin of the current COVID-19 strain of coronavirus by name, saying it had 'pandemic potential'." A high-level simulation was run in October 2019. Though China released the crucial information about the virus expeditiously, it did not reveal the extent of the epidemic for several weeks. But it was no secret to US intelligence, which was providing ominous warnings to the government through January and February. US officials familiar with the intelligence reports informed the press that "Donald Trump may not have been expecting this, but a lot of other people in the government were—they just couldn't get him to do anything about it. The system was blinking red."[16]

16 Harris, Shane, Greg Miller, Josh Dawsey, and Ellen Nakashima. "U.S. Intelligence Reports from January and February Warned about a Likely Pandemic." *Washington Post*. Accessed November 13, 2020. https://www.washingtonpost.com/national-security/us-intelligence-reports-from-january-and-february-warned-about-a-likely-pandemic/2020/03/20/299d8cda-6ad5-11ea-b5f1-a5a804158597_story.html.

Unfortunately, Fox and Friends didn't pick it up, so how could poor Donald know?

Countries in China's periphery reacted effectively. Most of Europe disregarded the information from China until it was too late. Well-organized societies with substantial diagnostic capacity and spare facilities (Germany, Norway) seem to have fared much better. Germany's death rate is far below others: 0.4%. "The biggest reason for the difference, infectious disease experts say, is Germany's work in the early days of its outbreak to track, test and contain infection clusters."[17] The United Kingdom has been one of the worst. The United States moved quickly to the rear of the pack.

It was quite instructive to compare Angela Merkel's clear, factual, considered report to the German people with the spectacle in Washington. A depressing picture of what Trump and his minions have done to the country.

As Trump's ineptitude and posturing drove the country to greater dangers, his approval rating "jumped by 5 points in the latest Gallup survey, matching the high point of his presidency, as a majority of voters say they have a positive view of how the president has

---

17 Morris, Loveday. "Why Germany's Coronavirus Death Rate Is so Much Lower than Other Countries' Rates." *Washington Post.* Accessed November 13, 2020. https://www.washingtonpost.com/world/europe/germany-coronavirus-death-rate/2020/03/24/76ce18e4-6d05-11ea-a156-0048b62cdb51_story.html.

handled the coronavirus pandemic." Approval was near unanimous among Republicans, whose primary news source is Fox News, studies show (along with Rush Limbaugh and Breitbart). It is perhaps not surprising, then, that as of mid-March, with the United States poised to become the epicenter of global crisis, a stunning 56% of Fox viewers believe that the media have "Greatly exaggerated the risks"—as compared with 25% of CNN viewers, which is bad enough.[18]

Trump may be ruining the country but there is no denying his skill as a conjurer, with effects that won't disappear quickly—and might intensify. That poses a significant challenge to activists, who have their work cut out for them.

To further ensure that the pandemic would spread at home, Trump's Department of Homeland Security began enforcing the largely inactive Public Charge Rule the day before the government warned of the coronavirus threat. The rule bans permanent residency to people who might become a public charge. The new Trump version extends its scope far more

18   Rowland, Geoffrey. "Gallup: Trump Job Approval Rating Matches All-Time High." Text. *The Hill*, March 24, 2020. https://thehill.com/homenews/administration/489285-gallup-trump-job-approval-rating-matches-all-time-high.

Pew Research Center. "American News Pathways: Explore the Data." Accessed November 13, 2020. https://www.pewresearch.org/pathways-2020/.

widely than before to include people who receive Medicaid and other benefits. Likely consequences are not hard to imagine: to avoid being identified as a public charge, millions of non-citizens are expected to disenroll from Medicaid. Just as testing and treatment are needed, many people will avoid health care for fear of being denied permanent residency and deported.[19]

A brilliant way to turn a threat into a potential catastrophe—and an illustration of how "security for the population" ranks against higher goals—in this case arousing fear of immigrants so that the frightened population will seek protection by the tough guy who is their savior.

Trump is also ensuring maximal suffering among official enemies, using the savage weapon of sanctions, third-party sanctions since no one dares defy the master. This form of torture is a virtually unique possession of the global hegemon. Cuba is resilient, having been subjected to US terror and economic strangulation since it became independent and engaged in "successful defiance" of US demands, the official designation of the crime. It is not only coping, but is providing medical assistance to others, an incredible irony. Members of the "European Union" are too weak and impoverished to help one another

19 Parmet, Wendy E. "Trump's Immigration Policies Weaken Our Ability to Fight Coronavirus." STAT (blog), March 4, 2020. https://www.statnews.com/2020/03/04/immigration-policies-weaken-ability-to-fight-coronavirus/.

but at least they can turn to the superpower across the Atlantic to come to their rescue. The Trump campaign to punish the people of Iran is turning crisis to catastrophe, as intended, apparently Venezuela as well. But even without the intense US commitment to induce maximal suffering, the poorer countries of the world are sure to be the most miserable victims, along with the more vulnerable at home.

In the main establishment journal, *Foreign Affairs*, Daron Acemoglu, who has studied how democracies die, writes that while Trump deserves blame for his disastrous reaction to the coronavirus crisis, "even more blameworthy has been the president's assault on US institutions, which began long before the novel coronavirus appeared and will be felt long after it is gone." He is referring to his systematic demolition of "the norms of professionalism, independence, and technocratic expertise" that make it possible for governments to function, while "prioritizing political loyalty above all else." By so doing, he is driving the country to the model of "autocratic states that offer little room for democratic input or criticism of government—and exhibit paper-thin policymaking competence as a result," incapable of reacting competently to crisis. As we see dramatically today.[20]

20 Acemoglu, Daron. "The Coronavirus Exposed America's Authoritarian Turn." *Foreign Affairs*, March 23, 2020. https://www.foreignaffairs.com/articles/2020-03-23/coronavirus-exposed-americas-authoritarian-turn.

It is a real achievement to lead the way to intensifying all three of the grim threats to survival that moved the setting of the Doomsday Clock closer to midnight than it has ever been.

Failure to respond adequately to the crisis cannot be attributed solely to Trump's wrecking ball. As we have seen, the roots are far deeper. In words that resonate in the United States, British human rights lawyer Afua Hirsch writes that

> This pandemic has exposed what many of us [in Britain] said about the Tories' long boast of 'record high' numbers of people in employment – namely, insecure workers with no rights and no safety net. Likewise, we warned about starving the NHS so that its resilience is shot, creating a generation of renters with no savings, and allowing homelessness and destitution to mushroom.[21]

The crisis has brought to the fore deep pathologies of modern society. The neoliberal onslaught has created dysfunctional governments unresponsive to the public along with a highly fragile international economy and a huge precariat, rendering official unemployment figures highly misleading. European austerity

21 Hirsch, Afua. "The Coronavirus Pandemic Threatens a Crisis for Human Rights Too." *The Guardian*, March 19, 2020. https://www.theguardian.com/commentisfree/2020/mar/19/coronavirus-pandemic-human-rights.

programs, imposed with little if any economic justifi-
cation, have added their share of suffering, engender-
ing justified anger and resentment, readily exploited
by demagogues. The system works well for the rich
until it gets some blow, at which point it falls apart—
as it did in 2008, far more so this time around. At the
very least the vast market failure over many years provides a powerful reason, if another one was needed, for
enacting universal health care, guaranteed sick leave,
and other minimal aspects of functioning society.

The profound failures should also lead to serious
reflection on what kind of world we want. The body
blow might just wake us up to understand that we
have to change course and cure the deeper pathology
of institutional structures designed for profit for the
few but not for human rights and needs, or even for
"survival of humanity" to borrow again the words of
the JPMorgan Chase memorandum cited earlier.

The same source unintentionally provided some
good advice to activists. It warns of "the financial and reputational risks of continued funding of
carbon-intensive industries, such as oil and gas." The
reputational risks are imposed by dedicated activism,
which, even short of institutional change, can induce
the masters of the universe to change course. History provides many examples. That is, to be sure, not
enough. But it provides some breathing space for the
much deeper reconstruction of the social order that is
needed for the survival of humanity in the dual sense:
survival of people and of human values.

The pandemic, for all its horrors, has a silver lining. It has brought to popular consciousness some of the roots of a wide range of social maladies, and exposed them to challenge. It has revealed the human qualities that can open the way to a much better world. The courage and dedication of health workers, often with barely minimal facilities and protection, is truly inspiring. The same is true of the ways that communities have been organizing to help those in need and to fill the spaces left by failing institutions. The shift in values from personal gain to mutual aid could be a basis for broad changes of consciousness with far-reaching import. They are also taking organizational form in promising ways. In Europe, DiEM25 is offering valuable ideas for confronting today's crises and working at grassroots and electoral levels to salvage what is of value in the European Union while overcoming its deep flaws, offering a wide range of opportunities for activists. Moving beyond, the founder of DiEM25, Yanis Varoufakis, has joined with Bernie Sanders in issuing a call for a progressive international to confront and overcome the international of reactionary states taking shape under the leadership of the criminal gang occupying the White House—temporary residents, if the population rises in time.

In the United States, activist movements have provided dramatic examples of what can be achieved. To take just one case, a green new deal, in some form, is essential for survival. A few years ago it was hardly more than an object of mainstream ridicule. Today it is firmly on the legislative agenda, the achievement of the young activists of the Sunrise Movement, whose efforts culminated in sit-ins in congressional offices, supported by young legislators whose electoral success owed a good deal to the popular activism inspired by Bernie Sanders.

This only skims the surface. It is the right time to keep firmly in mind the slogan that Gramsci made famous: Pessimism of the intellect, optimism of the will. And to act on it, forcefully and decisively. Anything less will be a fateful error.

Part 4

Reflections from Activists

At the beginning of 2020 we reached out to a few activists who have worked directly with Noam. We asked them to share their thoughts and experiences of having traveled the same road with Noam for various periods of time over the past 50 or 60 years. Although the reflections we gathered are by no means a methodical survey of the thousands of activists grateful to Noam for the direction and encouragement they received over these decades, we believe that they give us an insight into Noam Chomsky—the activist, the author, the intellectual, the man, and our colleague— that many might not otherwise experience. Perhaps in direct contradiction with Noam's desire to speak to our intellects, these anecdotes and reflections reveal that he has also spoken to our morale, our sense of purpose.... our hearts.

We start this final section of this book with an interview that Charlie Derber conducted with the well-known actor, Wallace Shawn (among his many credits, *My Dinner with Andre*). We feel that Wally captures some key elements of Noam's impact on many of us in a simple but profound way.

14 Making Me Feel that I Could Join with Others

Wallace Shawn and Charles Derber

CHARLIE DERBER: Well, Wally, my name is Charlie Derber. I teach sociology at Boston College. I'm just really thrilled to meet you and to have this chance to have a little bit of conversation with you about your encounters with Noam, and how they've shaped you, and so forth. Maybe you should introduce yourself just a little bit.

WALLY: I don't know how to characterize myself. I suppose I think of myself as a writer, and others can think of me any way they like.

CHARLIE: Wally, you're well known. 15 minutes ago, when we were sitting out on the street and having a little chat in the café, a number of people heard your voice, and stopped, and ran over to ask whether they could get a picture with you.

I wonder if you could tell me a little bit about your initial introduction to Noam, how you learned of Noam, when you met him, and just how that happened.

WALLY: Well, I met Noam in the '80s. I was a little over 40 and going through some kind of spiritual crisis,

Breaking away from my liberal roots, I suppose I'd always thought of the United States as basically a benevolent land of friendly people who sometimes were misled or had bad rulers, did bad things, but fundamentally, we were a decent people. I didn't have much awareness of my own role in the world, except I voted and read the newspaper. I don't know. As I got into my '40s, I went through psychological changes. I also was, really for the only time in my life, earning some good salary checks and paying taxes, so I became aware of my own role, for various reasons, in supporting whatever it was that my government was doing. I came to be aware of being a member of a certain class. I'd been brought up in privilege, and now with these checks, I was returning to privilege, at least for a while. I suddenly saw myself as a participant in the crimes of my own country and saw that my class was benefiting from torture, murder, things like that.

My girlfriend, also a writer, Deborah Eisenberg, gave me Noam's book that he wrote with Edward Herman, *The Political Economy of Human Rights*, the two volumes.

CHARLIE: Yeah, that was back in the '70s, I guess, that that was written.

WALLY: It might have been, but I probably got hold of it, I don't know, in the late 1980s. I totally freaked out, because I thought wow, this is all the stuff that I think I'm discovering, and he already discovered

it. He's described it so beautifully, and so forcefully, and so wittily, in a way. I mean, I loved the
way it was written. I was laughing out loud at his
marvelous irony, even as I was mourning the facts
that he was handing over. I loved the wonderful
footnotes, and I loved the encyclopedic thorough-
ness with which he argued his case. It was a pretty
joyful experience in a time when I was very, very
miserable, to discover what I was discovering and
to hate myself and my class, as I was coming to do.

I thought why not? I'll write him a letter. Why shouldn't
I? I had no introduction to him. I didn't know anybody
who knew him. I just wrote out of the blue, put a stamp
on the letter, sent it to Noam Chomsky at MIT. I said,
basically, I don't know how you can live without going
insane, walking through the world knowing what you
know. Now I'm coming to know these things, too, and
I don't know how I can handle it. I don't know how I
can walk around knowing these things. Maybe I should
leave the country, and maybe I should give up my citizenship. I don't want to participate in these crimes.
    Amazingly, he wrote back, and he said, "Well,
come to my office, and we can talk about this." Why?
Why should he do that? I think he feels that that's part
of his destiny or his mandate, to meet with tortured
souls such as me. I did go to see him. It was a very
moving experience, because, well, he was so kind.
He somewhat shocked me by saying, "But there are
a million things that you can do. Why would you

give up your citizenship and leave the country? This is where the fight is. That would be ludicrous." He sort of clued me into the fact that there was a big struggle going on, as it had been for years, but I had been too, you know, propagandized or too dumb to get it, really. I was invited to participate. Yes, I was participating on the evil side by paying my taxes, but perhaps I could participate on the good side in some way.

Of course, I also was inspired by the man, because he was knocking himself out devoting his life to trying to create a better world. That was moving.

CHARLIE: Am I right that this conversation was a catalyst for you?

WALLY: I know that before I'd met Noam, I'd been doing a certain amount of reading about the world. I did study history when I was a student, but it was all very abstract to me. It all changed when I saw my own part in it. Let's put it that way. The study of history was very abstract to me. By the way, it was taught in an abstract manner. I didn't get the human suffering that was going on behind these abstract terms. There was this empire, and there was this kingdom, and there was a balance of power, and there was this and that. I didn't quite get the human anguish lying behind all of that.

CHARLIE: Had you engaged in any kind of political activism prior to meeting Noam?

WALLY: Just the idea of activism, I felt that was for other people. I found it distasteful, the thought of being in a demonstration and chanting. Over the years, I have done some of those things that I didn't feel like doing, and I hope I will have the nerve to do more than I've done. I would never hold myself out as even a vaguely adequate person. I'm way inadequate. I think meeting Noam did have an influence on making me feel that I could join with others to, you know, behave differently.

Old South Church, Boston, October 19, 2016. Wally Shawn, Valeria Chomsky, Noam Chomsky and Angela Kelly on the occasion of Chomsky's "Internationalism or Extinction" presentation to 700 attendees
Photo by Paul Shannon.

CHARLIE: I'm struck by how personal your reaction is. A lot of people think of Noam Chomsky, he's a linguist, he's a theorist. He's making these sweeping analytical critiques of capitalism and global American hegemony, and I'm struck by how much this encounter with Noam, it impacted you in a very emotional and personal way.

WALLY: Well, his writing is based on tremendous compassion, but he writes without sentimentality. He commits the inexcusable crime of not giving the United States the benefit of the doubt, not sort of saying, "Well, of course we're nice guys, but…" He sort of questions the premise of whether we are nice guys. I think that's inadmissible.

CHARLIE: Absolutely. He's sort of speaking as a citizen of the world, and so he doesn't give America cover of any kind for the crimes and all the exploitation that he describes.

WALLY: I think that's one of the main reasons why he remains someone who could not be called for comment on the day's events by CNN, or CBS, or the normal news. Whereas, if you go to England or to Canada, just across the border, and go to Toronto, he's one of the people that if something happens, they'll call him up and ask his opinion. Here, he can talk with Amy Goodman, and otherwise, he can't talk with anybody.

CHARLIE: Yeah, you put your finger on it Wally, on why that is, which is that he speaks with a global voice, without any of what he would call the "necessary illusions" that American citizens and the media are expected to maintain about American exceptionalism.

WALLY: Because the reality of what we're doing in the world is so extreme, and because except for the blowing up of the World Trade Center, we don't have any effects of it. I mean, American life is unbelievably bland and peaceful compared to the life of countries that we have intervened in, such as Iraq or Vietnam. I mean, it's just unimaginable how monstrous the crimes are and how little price we've paid for them.

I was interviewed myself by the *New York Times*. I'm trying to think of when it was. It was probably 19... I don't know. I simply don't remember, but it was 15 years ago or something like that. The interviewer asked me, "Well, could you summarize..." We were talking about the theater or whatever. The interviewer said, "What are your political beliefs?"

I said, "Well, you know, it calls for a lengthy answer, but basically, I believe the things that... If you wanted to get a simple answer, I would say that I sort of believe most of everything that Noam Chomsky believe. So, if you read his books, you'll have a pretty good idea of most of what I believe." Then, the fact checker called me checking. I said, "Wait a minute." They read me what I myself had said. I said, "Wait a minute, you left out what I said about Noam Chomsky." They said, "No, no, we can't have that."

I said, "What do you mean you can't have that? The interviewer asked me about my political views, and I said that they were very similar to the views of Professor Chomsky. Can't I say that?" "No, you can't."

This was in the *New York Times*. I said, "Could I talk to your commanding officer and find out what you're telling me?" They said, "Well, we just can't keep... There was a hockey player who described three months ago how he was inspired by Noam Chomsky. We can't keep sort of promoting this one individual. You know, it was only three months ago that the hockey player mentioned Chomsky, and now you're mentioning him. We can't keep putting this in the *New York Times*."

Old South Church, Boston, April 11, 2019. Noam Chomsky and Amy Goodman presentation on the 3 greatest dangers facing humanity.

Photo by Pat Westwater-Jong

CHARLIE: But what about the world of theater and art? Is Chomsky's work known among... You know a large number of playwrights, and film writers, and actors, and so forth.

I'm just curious how, because you're a person of the theater and of words and of art, how you experience Noam from that perspective and from that world and whether you think that world has closed itself off as fully as the mass media has to Noam's very kind of unsettling message about the nature of the country?

WALLY: I am surprised by how many people I meet in the world of theater or film who have actually read him.

I think that his writing is not like one more book that you can read casually. If you read his political writing, you either have to say, "Well, I just think this is all wrong. I mean, I don't agree." Or you have to think can that be true? If you think it is true, then you see your life differently. He does sort of paint a very large picture. You're in the picture, if you read it intelligently.

It's quite heavy. You have to be prepared for that psychologically. You won't take it on unless you're ready, really. I mean, for me, it was just incredibly helpful to me. I was thinking oh gosh, could this be true? To myself, before I'd ever read Chomsky, I was thinking could that be true? Could this be true?

Could we really be like this? Could I really be like this? Then, to have this person who you have to respect... You know, by the time you've read a few pages of his writing, you sort of say, "Oh, well, this is someone I respect." To say, "Oh yes, that is true." You've described it in your head as a confused way. Now, I'm going to put it down on paper in a much better way. That was very helpful.

CHARLIE: Wally, thank you so much. This has really been very, very interesting.

WALLY: Thank you.

15 I'm a Citizen of the United States and I Have a Share of Responsibility for What It Does

Medea Benjamin

As a young woman, I was drawn to Latin America. I hitchhiked up and down the continent, soaking up the culture, the language, the strong sense of community. But I was confused by the anti-American sentiment I often encountered among young radicals I met. Searching for answers, I returned to the United States in 1973, just at the time of the coup against Salvador Allende in Chile. A friend sent me the writings of Noam Chomsky and it all became clear. I learned how the US government had tried to stop Allende from winning the elections, how the CIA was instructed to "make the economy scream," and how the US tragically rewarded the brutal military junta that reversed Chilean democracy and ushered in a reign of fascist terror. Chomsky made me understand the pattern of US policy—how it was designed to crush any alternatives, from Guatemala and Iran to Vietnam.

But Chomsky didn't just give me elements for critical analysis. He made me understand that it wasn't enough to just educate yourself, you had to do something—to take action. This is a lesson that has guided my life's trajectory. The other lesson is that while we may be critical of other governments, it is the responsibility of US citizens to focus on the role of our own government. "I'm a citizen of the United States and I have a share of responsibility for what it does," Chomsky said in *Deterring Democracy.* "I'd like to see it act in ways that meet decent moral standards." He made it clear that as US citizens, we have little influence over the politics of other nations, but we SHOULD have some influence over the actions of our own government. This, too, has guided me over the years as I have made decisions on where to focus my energies. Chomsky has been a great teacher and a moral guide.

16 What Chomsky Taught Me about Militancy

Ross Caputi

My first communication with Noam Chomsky was by email. I was a confused veteran, recently returned from Iraq. I had read a few introductory leftist texts, including Chomsky and Herman's *Manufacturing Consent*. My head was swimming with half-formed thoughts and self-doubt. I decided to write Chomsky, asking a set of embarrassingly naive questions. To my surprise, he responded *that day*. His words were reassuring and encouraging, and it meant the world to me.

A year or two later, several friends and I organized the Justice for Fallujah Project and we invited Chomsky to speak at our launch. He agreed, and I feel a bit silly admitting that I was surprised that Chomsky didn't ask for an honorarium and that he even took the subway to the event. Of course, he was a normal human being like the rest of us. I guess I was expecting an entourage. But Chomsky showed up alone and mingled dutifully before the event. And he was mobbed. Everyone wanted a moment with him. But he listened to everyone, nodded and smiled politely, and said a few choice and encouraging words when he could.

London, December 10, 2002. Chomsky speaks at Stop the War in Iraq meeting.
Photo by Photofusion/Universal Images Group via Getty Images.

Over the years, I approached Chomsky with a few other requests, and he always said "yes." Knowing well the power of his name, he lent it out generously to causes he believed in. On one occasion, I requested an interview about ongoing events in Iraq. We fixed an appointment, and I showed up a bit early with friends helping behind the camera. Journalists, filmmakers, students, and activists were lined up outside his door, and they flowed in and out incessantly, in near half-hour intervals. When our appointment came, we set up the camera quickly, completed the interview, and broke down the equipment early—we wouldn't take any time that wasn't ours. To our surprise, Chomsky's secretary told us that we might be the first group ever *not* to have stolen a few extra minutes.

By then I got it. We all needed Chomsky desperately and everyone was constantly looking to him for answers, for a moment of his time, or for a brush with genius. And he accepted that role. His gifted mind helped us understand the world we live in, and, in doing so, he empowered us. Chomsky made me realize that I had first learned from him the importance of sound analysis when speaking out, but I was late in coming to appreciate the *social* importance of being a community organizer. Chomsky showed me a new, deeper understanding of the role. True militancy means saying "yes" as often as possible to those who need you. It means being patient and kind to others, and maintaining a generosity of spirit, even when you're exhausted. Chomsky has given me so much, through his writings and in our few face-to-face encounters, but I think this is the most important thing I learned from him.

17 Celebrating Chomsky

Challenging the Opposition to History

Bill Fletcher, Jr.

The United States has a peculiar characteristic: it openly opposes history and, instead, embraces myth. The established order goes out of its way to dismiss, if not obliterate, facts that run contrary to dominant, capitalist myth. And those who offer such a challenge do so at the risk of facing the wrath of the Gorgon.

Noam Chomsky's single greatest contribution has been his unwavering willingness to challenge the dominant myth about the nature, functioning and foreign policies of the capitalist formation known as the United States of America. He has repeatedly done so with devastating detail and acuity. Whether he is discussing the Israeli/Palestinian conflict, or US de-stabilization efforts in Latin America, he offers much more than an informed opinion. Rather, he offers up facts and a storyline that ties the facts together, thus making sense of a situation and helping the reader or observer to better understand *the* connections be-tween events, and the connection between events and socio-economic systems.

In taking on this role, Chomsky runs up against what I would argue is the dominant approach to history and accountability in the United States: I call it "from now on." It is a simple framework and has been highly successful. It goes like this: *the USA may have committed any number of crimes over its history, from enslavement of Africans to genocide against Native Americans to atrocious conditions for working-class people of all colors…but none of that matters because it was in the past. Therefore, from now on, we—of the USA—will commit to be better people. We will not apologize for anything. We will not return anything that we stole or compensate anyone for any deaths attributable to our actions. We will just commit to not do it again.*

The life and work of Noam Chomsky has stood in opposition to such an approach. He has made history and current events relevant to us all. But he has also insisted on something very unpopular: we, in the United States, cannot hide behind the drapes of our alleged ignorance. We cannot pretend that we were unaware of this or that action by our government or by the corporations of global capitalism, using such an alleged lack of awareness to shield us from responsibility. We cannot say that we "…did not know…" After being exposed to the work of Noam Chomsky, and those who have emulated him, we are faced with either taking progressive action or admitting, in our heart, that we knew what we wanted to know, and, yes, we are comfortable being complicit in the larger crime.

18 Never Meet Your Heroes?

Charngchi Way

Years ago, I had some complications at work, which made my housing situation precarious. I was couch surfing for a while. I had gotten to know Noam and the staff at MIT pretty well in the few years living and working in Boston, and had the chance to drive him to talks a few times. When Noam's assistant Bev heard about my housing situation, she brought it up with Noam at the office and sort of gave him a nudge.

So there I was, staying at Noam Chomsky's house for the summer. This was a year after his first wife, Carol, had passed away. He would mention her often in passing in sweet but somber tones. Living alone after all these years I think he welcomed the company. During the summers he would stay at the Cape Cod house and the Lexington house on alternate weeks. I got to see Noam's process up close.

During breakfast and morning coffee, he would read through three newspapers: the *New York Times* ("The most important newspaper in the United States, and one can argue, in the world."), the *Wall Street Journal* ("Great business reporting, and the best comic strip in the country (referring to the editorials)"), and the

Financial Times ("The only paper that tells the truth"). Noam is an active reader, with a pen in hand, marking up the articles, a quote here, a source there. He insists that he does not speed read, but I suspect that his ability to absorb information at such pace sets him apart from mere mortals.

Two days a week he would go into the MIT office for a day of appointments: interviews with the media, advising students, meetings with activists. Bev runs a tight ship knowing how precious Noam's time is, but invariably he would run long, because he takes everyone seriously.

The rest of the week, he would work in his home office, going back and forth between answering email inquiries and doing his own writing and research tasks. Aside from the occasional bathroom breaks he wouldn't budge from the keyboard.

Late afternoons, he takes a walk around the neighborhood, through the woods behind his house if the weather permits, enjoying the fresh air, and mingling with the neighbors.

After a simple dinner, he pours a glass of whiskey, and sits down in the living room reading professional journals, one of dozens he gets in the mail, or one of the books from his ever-growing piles around the house and in his office. Marking it up and going through them with the same intensity and speed as the newspapers.

After a while, he gets back on the computer, answering more email inquiries and other tasks. Usually a bit past midnight, he'll emerge from his office with a smile and tells me he will knockoff and going to sleep for the night. As a much younger person, I can't imagine having the same commitment to such a schedule. It exhausts me just recounting it here.

He would occasionally break from his rigid schedule, like one week when he found out a friend and prominent person from the Vietnam era will be on a TV retrospective on the Vietnam War. He was interested and asked me to find when and what channel it is on so we can watch it together. We sat down and not even 15 minutes into the special, he stood up and shook his head disappointedly and told me with a sigh, that the program is still stuck in the liberal framing of the war as a mistake, as opposed to it having been immoral and wrong.

He went back to doing work in his home office. There were many other personal memories that summer, it's something I'll always remember. They say that you should never meet your heroes because they are sure to disappoint you. I think there are always exceptions. Noam Chomsky is one of them.

19 So We Turned to Noam

Sandra Ruiz Harris

Before I came to the United States, I knew of Noam Chomsky's reputation as a formidable critic of his country's policies toward Latin America. Arriving in Boston and getting involved with solidarity activism and pro-immigrant work, I was surprised to find that local activists had such ready access to him. Not only was he someone that they could turn to as a thinker and as the conscience of a nation, but he was also accessible in ways that mattered for activists. He was always ready to join a rally, speak at public events, and sign onto many petitions and public calls to action. For a project that I have helped build since 2006, encuentro5, a multi-organizational collaborative space for organizing, debating, and base of operations right in downtown Boston, this was a matter of life and death: late in its first year, struggling to pay the commercial rents that our city's landlords demanded, we had reached a crisis point—not enough money to make rent and not much more predicted to come in over the next few months. So we turned to Noam. He readily agreed to speak at a public event—one for which we could solicit donations from the attendees.

The event attracted the predictable hundreds of participants, some paying $50 to attend a pre-event reception for which Noam also generously gave of his time. By the end of the event, our organization was solvent for many months to come. Nearly every year thereafter, Noam spoke at a large public gathering that we helped organize and that benefited our organization and the scores of other organizations that now use our space as an organizing platform. After each event, we'd send Noam a brief thank you and a note about how much we raised, how many people attended, and the results of our activist "asks." By the next morning, a simple reply would follow to the effect of, "I am glad that the event worked out for you."

20 Never Lose Faith in Humanity

Robert W. McChesney

I first saw Noam Chomsky speak in 1986 and it changed my life. His intellectual honesty and courage were and are striking, in an intellectual culture where both are in short supply. He never focus-grouped his ideas to see what would be most convincing. He just told the truth as he saw it, and assumed others could make up their own minds. The core lesson Noam taught me was to never lose faith in humanity, and in the ability of people to change the world and live together in harmony. He rejection of elitism, his embrace of genuine democracy, his ability to entertain an idea without accepting it, his humility, are all embedded in his bone marrow. Instantly when one reads him or hears him speak, you get it that Noam is speaking the truth, and he has a heart as robust as his mind. I have learned so much from him, like so many others, and we must all try to pass it along.

Boulder, Colorado, April 2003. Chomsky speaks at anti-war rally soon after the start of the Iraq War.

Photo By Karl Gehring/*The Denver Post* via Getty Images

21 Strengthening the Spirit of Middle East Activists

Nancy Murray

I made my first visit to the occupied West Bank and Gaza Strip in 1988 near the start of the Intifada. What I witnessed made me determined to set up an organization that would work to change US policy toward Israel/Palestine.

When I asked Professor Chomsky if he would join the advisory committee of The Middle East Justice Network (MEJN), he said he would be helpful when called upon, but if we were serious about building an effective organization we should not include his name. Raising the profile of the Palestinian struggle in the 1970s and 1980s had already made him a pariah in many circles.

Shrugging off personal vilification, Noam repeatedly answered our call to speak at our annual conferences. In 1993, he keynoted our conference in Wichita, Kansas, a trip requiring long hours and three plane changes. His commitment to reach new audiences, and the generosity with which he gave his time—without expecting any recompense—were all the more remarkable given how extraordinarily busy he was.

Nancy Murray and Noam await their turn to speak.
Photo by Pat Westwater-Jong.

As co-founder of the Gaza Mental Health Foundation, I am especially grateful for the numerous talks
he gave on the Gaza Strip following the imposition of
the Israel's blockade in 2007 and its subsequent military aggressions. In December 2009, pressure placed
on a Newton church forced an event about Gaza at
which we were both scheduled to speak to be re-
located with just two days' notice.

In 1989 my daughter, then a high school student,
traveled to the occupied territories with a MEJN delegation. On her return, she wrote an article for a local paper describing how the Israeli army raided the

house in a Gaza Strip refugee camp where she was spending the night.

She was not prepared for the scores of letters excoriating her and her article in the weeks following its publication. One (unsolicited) letter she received at home made her feel much better. It was a lengthy one from Noam, who explained that a pro-Israel group called CAMERA had seen her article and organized all those opposing letters to deter other young people from thinking too deeply about the issue. The time and care he took to both educate her and strengthen her spirit reflect his dedication to the cause, his empathy, and his gift as a teacher.

22 Human Freedoms are not Gift from Above

Norman Solomon

Ever since I first encountered his writing and public speaking in the early 1980s, Noam has been a profound model and inspiration—showing how key facts, cogent analysis, and determined activism need each other. In the process, Noam has exemplified how being in solidarity with movements for social justice must involve being distinctly out of step with powers-that-be in realms of media, government, and academia. Effective activism requires a sense of urgency and a long view, to put out destructive fires and plant seeds for what we might not live to see. Noam has been providing tremendous illumination in that zone. Through it all, he underscores in countless ways that human freedoms are "never a gift from above." Whether more than 30 years ago, when I was reading books like his *Turning the Tide* and hearing him on a community radio station—or whether these days I read a transcript of a new interview with Noam online—his clarity has shined intense light on paths ahead.

23 Puncturing the Wall of Lies and Deception

Mark Solomon

It was perhaps the early '80s. Hundreds converged on storied Stuyvesant High School in New York City, filling the auditorium to overflowing—protesting the latest Israeli outrage against occupied Palestine. I had been asked to join a panel discussion with Noam Chomsky and a third participant whom I no longer recall. For some unfathomable reason, the organizers of the program slotted me to speak last, with Chomsky preceding me.

As usual, Chomsky mesmerized the audience with an array of facts drawn from massive reading and delivered in a softly modulated voice that without bombast or pandering fully engaged the audience. He punctured the wall of lies and deception that characterized what we now refer to as the mainstream media. There were the facts often resurrected from arcane places; there was searing analysis and most important, there was intense moral urgency that literally spoke truth to power.

So there we were, again sharing a platform, with me close enough to see his notes scribbled on what appeared to be the back of an envelope, turning those notes into a brilliant exposure of calumnies and falsehoods permeating the Palestinian-Israeli conflict.

When Chomsky concluded, something happened. The audience of hundreds nearly disappeared. It seemed like a sea of humanity flowed out of the hall. In that crowd surging toward the exits, I noticed a warmly familiar dark-haired woman. *My wife had joined the retreating throng.*

There I was—facing a bare quorum scattered around the auditorium. Whatever the remaining audience, I did my thing while feeling grateful for the opportunity to share a platform with one of the greatest minds and most politically effective figures in the present-day world.

24 Mind and Hearts Cracked Open

Chuck Collins

One of the great things about living in the Boston area, at least before he moved to Arizona, was the ability to regularly hear Noam Chomsky speak. Noam also invited me to speak about economic inequality at his MIT seminar periodically. Chomsky's seminars were a beehive of critical conversation. Seats were filled with eager students having their minds and hearts cracked open. But the wider community was also invited to attend and we did. Sometimes there were over 300 people wedged into the lecture hall.

One gift of Chomsky's presence is in the truly radical nature of his thinking—in the full meaning of the word—going to the roots. He is a vibrant systems thinker, making the connections across disciplines and compartmentalized knowledge. He invited and exhorted us—his students and the activist community—to go deeper in our analysis and understanding of social and economic problems—and to bring a deeply humanist and internationalist perspective to our actions.

Week after week, he lifted up the day's news from around the planet and provided a deeper historical and political analysis. Thousands of us learned to look beyond the surface headlines—and critically reflect on the daily diet served up by the corporate media.

25 He Has Never Stopped

Joseph Gerson

It has been my privilege to have worked on and off with Noam, among my most important teachers, models, and inspirations, off and on for the last four decades. Noam is a man who has had profound impacts on who we have become, how we see the world, and the actions we have taken for peace, justice, and environmental sustainability. It goes without saying that over the past half century with Noam's indefatigable thinking, writing, and speaking that he has nourished movements across the country and around the world.

Fifty years ago Fred Branfman, who exposed the covert bombing of Laos by the United States and served as the Director of Project Air War, wrote an article titled *When I Saw Noam Chomsky Cry*. It was about Noam's visit to Laos in 1970. Fred was an extraordinary figure, who lived among Laotians and documented the unprecedented and criminal six years of secret bombings of the people of the Plain of Jars in Laos. Fred heard the stories of "countless grandmothers burned alive by napalm, countless children buried alive by 500-pound bombs, parents shredded by anti-personnel bombs" in

Istanbul, Turkey, January 19, 2013. Chomsky speaks on the balcony of the offices of the Armenian paper, Agos, during commemoration ceremony for slain Armenian journalist Hrant Dink who was killed by a gunman in 2007.
Photo by MIRA/AFP via Getty Images.

a land that was transformed into a moonscape. Tens of thousands of peaceful villagers were killed or driven underground and into caves or into Vientiane, the Laotian capital city.

What stood out in Fred's memory was a meeting with Plain of Jars refugees. He was stunned when, while translating Noam's questions and the refugees' heart-rending answers, he saw Noam break down and begin weeping. It was then, Fred wrote, that he could see directly into Noam's soul.

Beyond, or maybe related to, Noam's intellect and his moral compass are his humility, his generosity of spirit and his common decency, to which I would add his intellectual and physical courage. Few people have driven themselves to publish as many books in any field, let along as many fields as Noam has. Yet, Noam has consistently made the time to speak at community-based movement building and fund raising events, and he has found the energy and will to work into the early morning hours answering inquiries sent to him from graduate students and others across the country and around the world who he has yet to meet.

Among the areas where Noam has provided us with path breaking history and analysis has been his work as a leading critic of Israeli and US Middle East policies. In 1969, two years after the Six-Day Middle East War, Noam wrote and published *Peace in the Middle East?* and co-founded the Committee on New Alternatives in the Middle East with a statement designed break the silence. That book and the statement paved the way for thousands who have since worked for Palestinian rights, for a just resolution to the Israeli–Palestinian conflict and who are now resisting the campaign to silence the Boycott, Divestment and Sanctions movement.

Noam was an outstanding critic of Ronald Reagan's Central American wars, and among the memories I cherish is being arrested with Noam and Howard Zinn when 500 of us closed the Federal Building in Boston to protest the Contra War.

Noam was the featured speaker in the country's first major peace movement conference following the 9–11 attacks and the US invasion of Afghanistan. His talk helped to break the fearful silence that many will remember prevailed in the months following those terrorist attacks. Let me invoke Einstein's observation that genius is 1% inspiration and 99% perspiration. I don't know if he got those proportions right, but they reflect just how hard and courageously Noam has worked to stop the killing and for peace, justice, and human survival. He has never stopped becoming and giving.

Contributors

Medea Benjamin is co-founder of CODEPINK and the fair trade advocacy group, Global Exchange. She is recipient of the 2014 Gandhi Peace Award among other honors. Her latest book is *Inside Iran: The Real History and Politics of the Islamic Republic of Iran.*

Ross Caputi, Marine Veteran, Co-Author, *The Sacking of Fallujah: A People's History.*

Chuck Collins is Director of the Program on Inequality at the Institute for Policy Studies. He is author of *Born on Third Base* and *Is Inequality in America Irreversible?*

Bill Fletcher, Jr. is the executive editor of globalafricanworker.com, the former president of TransAfrica Forum, and a long-time writer and labor movement activist.

Joseph Gerson is Director of Program for the Northeast Office of the American Friends Service Committee and Executive Director of the Campaign for Peace, Disarmament and Common Security.

Sandra Ruiz Harris is a Coordinator of encuentro5 and a member of Chelsea Uniting against the War (a community-based antiwar organization based in Chelsea, MA).

Robert W. McChesney, Media Activist, Professor of Communications.

Nancy Murray founded the Middle East Justice Network and co-founded the Gaza Mental Health Foundation. She is the past Director of The Bill of Rights Education Project for the ACLU of Massachusetts.

Wallace Shawn is an American actor, voice artist, comedian, playwright and essayist. His film roles have included those of Wally Shawn in the Louis Malle-directed drama My Dinner with Andre, Vizzini in The Princess Bride, and many others. Shawn is the author of books on theatre, politics and society, including *Essays, Night Thoughts*, and *Evening at the Talk House.*

Mark Solomon is Professor of History, Emeritus at Simmons University. He is a past national co-chair of the Committees of Correspondence for Democracy and Socialism.

Norman Solomon, Antiwar Activist, Journalist, former Congressional Candidate.

Charngchi Way is a long-time labor movement and media activist in the Boston area.

Index

Note: *italic* page numbers refer to figures.

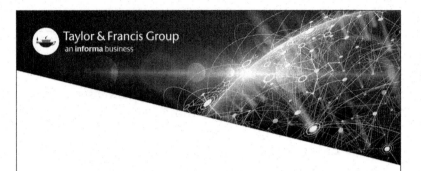